A Survival Guide for Truck Drivers

Tips from the Trenches

A Survival Guide for Truck Drivers

Tips from the Trenches

by Alice Adams and Andrew Ryder

Contributors: Ronald T. Adams
Kristin Paige Berthelsen

THOMSON
TM
DELMAR LEARNING

Australia   Canada   Mexico   Singapore
Spain   United Kingdom   United States

THOMSON

——✳——

DELMAR LEARNING

TM

A Survival Guide for Truck Drivers
by Alice Adams and Andrew Ryder

Business Unit Executive Director:
Susan L. Simpfenderfer

Executive Production Manager:
Wendy A. Troeger

Executive Marketing Manager:
Donna J. Lewis

Acquisitions Editor:
Paul Drougas

Cover Design:
Kristina Almquist

Channel Manager:
Wendy E. Mapstone

Developmental Editor:
Patricia Gillivan

NOTICE TO THE READER

Contents

Acknowledgments

The authors and Delmar Learning would like to express their gratitude to the following professionals whose suggestions helped us shape this book.

Kevin W. Burch, President
Jet Express, Inc.

Charles J. Mosqueda
Wichita Area Technical College

Taylor Squires
National Transportation Training and Consulting

Introduction

As a professional driver, you spend your days crossing the plains and valleys of the United States, Canada, and in some cases, Mexico. You and your fellow drivers continue a proud tradition of making America one of the greatest and strongest commercial centers in the world.

Your father may have taught you to drive your first truck. Or you may have learned on the job or attended a professional driving school. As you spend time on the road, you learn additional skills, skills that help you in your work and in living your life day to day. But the learning process doesn't end after six months or a year, or even five or 10 years.

Each day, you find you need more skills to cope with the demands placed on you, today's professional driver. There's more traffic, more construction, more road rage, and more stress. There is also more technology, new shippers to deal with, and in most cases, continuing challenges and issues at home and on the job.

You spend hours alone on the highway or on the streets of the community or region you serve. This book can be your companion, your guide, and your friend as you do your job day in and day out.

In the chapters ahead, you'll find the answers to these questions and more:

- How do you keep the lines of communication open with your customers, coworkers, and family members?

- How do you control your weight and blood pressure to avoid a career-ending illness?

- How do you apply to modern trucking what Paul learned about pecan pie in a small 1920s country cafe in a dusty Nebraska farming community?

- What are the time-proven and internationally accepted steps to deescalate a conflict with a coworker or customer?

- How do you reassure your family or your partner that you love them when you only see them a few days each month?

- How do you manage your money on the road?

- How do you handle the killer stress that builds up as you negotiate crowded streets and highways?

- What can you do to prevent your children from becoming aggressive drivers when they grow up?

You will find the answers to these and more questions about professional truck driving in the 21st century in this easy-to-read book written by people who know the trucking industry, and respect professional drivers and the jobs they do.

Read this book and shift your professional driving life skills into high gear. It will be time well spent.

Chapter 1

Making the Transition

When you choose a career as an over-the-road professional driver, you no longer have an 8 a.m. to 5 p.m. job. You may leave your family or loved ones for weeks on end. You will miss out on social opportunities and you will not be there for many family events. You will need to deal with setbacks and frustrations without losing your cool. You will experience periods of endless boredom. You may often feel lonely. In short, you will be making a major lifestyle change.

Making this change requires adjustments. If you aren't aware of what these are or you are unwilling to make them, you're in for a tough time. Relationships with your loved ones will suffer, you will be irritable and quick-tempered, and your job performance may decline.

Before becoming a professional driver, it's a good idea to talk to other drivers and their spouses to understand how they have adjusted. They often can tell stories about lessons they've learned. Here are a couple of stories from the wives of professional drivers.

> *Mark retired from a military career to become a professional driver. While he was in the military, he was not away from home for long periods of time, and he could take weekend*

trips to many interesting and fun places with his wife Mary and their children.

Mark was also home for most family events like Thanksgiving, Christmas, birthdays, and school events. He was also available for family emergencies.

Mary recalls how Mark became a driver. "My father-in-law, who is a truck driver, had been telling my husband for years that he should become a driver after he retired. So I quit a job I loved, we packed up, and moved to California where Mark went to truck driving school. My husband had worked in logistics in the military, so he did well in school and got a good paying, over-the-road job right away.

"One of the many things I admire about Mark is how dedicated he is to whatever he does. When he was in the military, Mark often won the base award for leadership. He was always the cleanest and sharpest. He is the same way about his driving. When he comes home, he always cleans his rig.

"The only problem with the driving job is that we feel like he abandoned us. No more being home for special occasions. I am actually a single parent because Mark is rarely home.

"The kids and I have had to learn that trucking isn't just a job for Mark. It is a way of life. When he first started driving, I was lucky if I could get him by phone. Now he has a cell phone and a computer, which make it easier for us to communicate at least once a day.

With a lot of planning, he has managed to be home for some holidays and major events in our kids' lives, like graduation. One graduated from high school and one from college.

"But the unexpected always happens when Mark is away. Like one kid wrecking three cars in two months. So I got to do all the "fun things," like rushing to the hospital after one of the wrecks, or dealing with the insurance company and then purchasing another vehicle, something I had never done.

When our plumbing cratered last summer, I was the one who had to find the money, hire the plumber, and deal with the bad news.

"When our kids went off to college, I thought things would get better. I planned to go on the road with my husband. It was kind of fun. But I didn't like the hurry, hurry all the time. We had to keep on schedule. It was, "Do you have to stay in the bathroom so long?" And "Can't you do your makeup later?"

"I only take short trips with Mark, now. I go out with friends maybe once a month or so, but I've really found that I need my "alone time." With the kids gone, I am only responsible for me. I have a job I love. I don't have to rush home from work to fix dinner or do the laundry.

"In a way, I have developed this double personality: the "single" me who does what I want to do when I want to do it; and the "married me" who cooks, cleans, and does all those other wifely things when Mark comes home.

"And it is hard on Mark, too. When he is in his truck, he is not accountable to anyone but his schedule. But when he comes home, he has all these chores to do like cut the grass and repair the fence. He has a family who demands his attention and he is so tired from working so many hours for so many days that all he wants to do is sleep."

Carrie is also married to a trucker who switched careers.

"We have a ten-year-old daughter and a six-year-old son," she says. "About three years ago, my husband worked in construction 60 to 70 hours a week. Between our one-hour commutes one-way, and his working those long hours, we didn't have much time for each other. In order to help our family and our finances, we decided we needed to move back to Texas, and that my husband would make a drastic career change and become a truck driver.

"After the move, my husband went to school and earned his commercial driver's license. He first worked as a company driver for a year and learned the ropes. I quickly learned while he was away attending truck driving school that I had my own "hoops" to jump through.

"The first and the worst challenge for me was loneliness. My husband and I had never been apart for more than a few nights during our 10 years together. I believe we may have taken each other for granted, so this experience really started to show me how much I loved and needed him. I cried every night for the six weeks he was away at truck driving school.

"Then he was home for a week, got hired as a company driver, and I had to take him to the bus station. And my crying began again. For about six months, every time he had to leave after his home time, I cried. I finally got to the point where I could say goodbye without tears, but it was a long, tough process.

"To make it worse, we did not have a cell phone, so I did not hear from him every night. Now that he has a cell phone, he calls me at least once a day, sometimes more. Sometimes our conversations are long, and sometimes they last just long enough for him to tell me that he's okay, parked for the night, and is going to bed.

"At first, I worried about everything. My husband had told me about the 'lot lizards,' which is slang for 'hookers.' They prowl the truck stop parking lots looking for business.

"Then, of course, there are road hazards such as bad weather, drivers with road rage, and road construction. I worried that my husband would slide off a mountain road in the snow or flip over and be injured. Another worry was money. Then there are the household worries: appliances acting up; a flat on the car; children and pets misbehaving.

"The way I've found to deal with all these worries is to have faith and to let others help if I need them. Another way I've found help is to find Web sites where there are other truckers' wives who are going through the same experiences I am. There is great comfort in having someone to talk to who *understands. I believe that only other truck drivers' wives can comprehend the worries and joys of our daily lives, will understand that this is the lifestyle we've chosen for our family, and won't look down on us for it."*

There are common threads through these two stories. Clearly, both the driver and his spouse must go through a period of personal adjustment, and there must be a willingness to make changes.

Making these changes requires five personal qualities.

1. *Patience*—To deal with uncertainties and things that are out of your control. Also, to deal with another's reluctance to change.

2. *Realistic Expectations*—Change is a process: it doesn't happen overnight. It's important to keep this in mind so that the bar isn't raised too high too early.

3. *Open Communication*—So there are no misconceptions where little things get turned into big things.

4. *Teamwork*—All parties (driver, partner, children) must agree to be in it together and function as a team. Without everyone's cooperation in areas such as time commitments and financial pressures, the adjustment is that much harder.

5. *Appreciation*—Thank others often for the part they are playing, even if your task may seem far more important or demanding.

In summary, you can make the transition to long-haul driving easier if you go into it knowing the challenges and pitfalls. Discuss these challenges with all those who currently have a stake in your personal time. At the very least, they should know how your new career will impact your relationships with them. Be aware of the role changes that will take place and make sure others are prepared to take them on.

Finally, remember that driving over-the-road is a tremendous commitment, and you, your family, and close friends will make a lot of sacrifices. These sacrifices will only be worth it if you can make the transition successfully.

JOIN THE FRATERNITY

After so many years, the faces you see when you stop regularly at one place or another become familiar. And that's how it was at the Cody Truckstop, stuck out in the middle of nowhere, its neon sign a welcoming beacon to drivers in the night.

Cody's was a place where you could come and join in the discussions—which usually ended up as debates—or you could be to yourself, over in the corner with your cup of java and your donuts or whatever.

"We don't know strangers," the owner once told me. "We're out here in the middle of the desert and we're just glad to see you when you come by. Everybody's welcome."

I had seen the owners give away food and bus fare to the homeless people who had hitched a ride and then been dumped in the middle of nowhere, and had walked to Cody's. I had also seen them—at 2 a.m. in the morning—help runaways get back to their families, talking and listening to youngsters, making phone calls for them, and finding them ways to get home.

That day in September when I stopped in at Cody's, a lot of familiar faces greeted me when I walked into the café. As usual, the tales were tall and the camaraderie was genuine.

About half way through the burger Cody's is famous for from coast to coast, one of the guys at the counter suddenly fell back on the floor. His eyes were wide open and his body was writhing. A second later, he was still, and his face was changing from pale to purple.

"Quick! He needs air! Who knows CPR?" yelled the waitress who had been chatting with the counter customers.

One of the truckers slipped out of a booth and began breathing into the guy's mouth, then pounding on his chest. Another had his cell phone out, calling for emergency help.

By the time the EMTs arrived, the driver on the floor had regained some color and the trucker administering CPR was more than ready for some relief. One of the truck stop's owners followed in his car behind the ambulance. And within 20 minutes, a phone call came, saying the customer had suffered a heart attack and the trucker who administered CPR had saved his life. Of course, that guy was long gone, headed down the highway toward Phoenix.

The truck stop owner, calling from the hospital, told us the guy was an owner-operator, worried about getting his load to the consignee's dock on time. One of the guys at Cody's called the shipper to let them know what had happened. And before we left Cody's that day, we'd set up a place where truckers could drop in some change to help the guy get back home and on his feet.

One of the guys at the counter, a local, offered to go out and lock up the rig.

A few weeks later, when I was by Cody's again, I heard that coworkers had come to take the truck to its destination so the freight would be delivered on time. The money donated at Cody's was enough to pay for the driver's wife to fly in and to drive her husband back home when he was released from the hospital.

Of course, the best news was that the trucker survived the heart attack and would eventually recover. But all of us were drawn together by the incident, and we left Cody's, knowing that if it had been one of us instead of him, we were in good company, a fraternity of sorts, a proud tradition that takes care of its own whatever the need might be.

Chapter 2

Being an Effective Communicator

You may be asking yourself, "Why do I need to read about communications? I've been doing it all of my life. I already know how to communicate!"

Of course you do. You began communicating shortly after you left the womb. Your cries and gurgles evolved into words and gestures, and then sentences and paragraphs. But how effective are you as a communicator today?

Being an effective communicator helps you become better at your profession, what you do day-to-day, week-to-week.

STEP ONE: STOP TALKING AND START LISTENING

Studies in the workplace have shown that certain problems keep reoccurring due to the lack of good communication skills.

A safety director for a large trucking company put it this way: "We tell our drivers, 'If you have a problem, if the load is going to be late, or if you have a breakdown, before you do anything else, call dispatch.'" The director then shook his head. "If one driver in 10 thinks about calling in when there's a problem, I feel really lucky."

As a professional driver, you need to know how to communicate effectively with other drivers, your dispatcher, the shop, your road manager, your customers, law enforcement personnel, and service providers along the highways you travel.

While it appears to be a simple process, effective communications is often a complex task because it can be complicated by a variety of personalities, moods, situations, and the goals of both the sender and the receiver of the message.

For example, if you're not a morning person and the phone rings early in the morning, the voice you use may be different than the tone you have later in the day. Or, if you've just had an argument with a significant other and the phone rings, your tone will be different than if you hadn't had the altercation.

Communication can be defined as the process where information is exchanged between or among individuals through a common system of symbols, signs, or behavior.

Early man, when approaching a stranger, would hold a shield in one hand and raise the other in greeting, showing that he didn't have a knife or a spear ready to throw. That sign or behavior was passed down through the centuries and today, we still use this sign of greeting except we no longer carrier shields and we call it a "wave."

We also use words—symbols—to express the ideas we want to get across to another person.

Because we communicate daily—even when we're on the road for hours at a time —and because it looks and sounds like a simple process, we sometimes forget about the things that may affect our communication such as our health, what kind of day we've had, how much sleep we got the night before, if Junior or Sissy had a good or not so good report card, if we're having trouble with the truck, or if we missed a load or were bumped in seniority.

How easy is it to communicate? A few weeks ago, John called a nearby pizzeria and ordered three pizzas for the gang: one pepperoni, one-half hamburger/one-half cheese, and one with everything except onions and Canadian bacon.

When the delivery man came to the door, he had one cheese pizza, one pepperoni, and one Canadian bacon and onion pizza.

Ever have that problem? Sure you have. The problem was communication. Either John's order was not stated in a clear and concise manner or the person taking the order wasn't listening.

That brings us to our next step in good communications: listening.

If you add up your total communication time for each day, you may be surprised to find that more than 75 percent of your waking hours is spent listening to your dispatcher, your boss, the shipper, the consignee, the CB, someone on your cell phone, the radio or CD, or an audiobook or tape. You'll also listen to the cashier at the fuel stop or the waitress at the truck stop where you have dinner.

Seventy-five percent of communication is simply listening. Yet we're not well trained in this area. In high school, a lot of students take speech courses or public speaking, but how many of us took listening classes?

You may be saying to yourself, "What's the big deal about listening? You just close your mouth and open your ears, right?"

Well, not quite. In fact, picture some of the stereotyped cartoons featuring a man reading the newspaper at the breakfast table while his wife talks on and on about a problem with the kids, the bills, or the PTA meeting next Friday. The guy's sitting there with his mouth shut and his ears open, but is he really listening? In fact, his attention is probably not on what his wife is saying but on what he's reading in the newspaper. So how much is he hearing? Maybe only every second or third word she's saying.

Is the guy reading the newspaper going to remember what he's being told? No. And how does this make his wife feel? Probably like she's not too important, right?

Listening can be defined as receiving information through what you hear and what you see. You then give meaning to the words or the pictures and decide what you think about it. Then you respond.

Sound simple? You're right! But we often make listening much more difficult than it is because we sometimes "half-listen" or we distort what we're hearing because we think we've heard it all before. Or sometimes we don't pay attention at all because we don't like the looks of the speaker or because our minds may be somewhere else.

As a professional driver, however, you may have only one chance to hear what your dispatcher or your customer is telling you, so it is important to put aside your personal "stuff" and really hear what they're saying.

Experts who have studied listening say it is a process requiring six individual steps.

1. *Preparation*—Knowing enough about what the speaker is talking about to understand what's being said. This may be the case when someone is giving you directions to a place you haven't been before. In this case, having a map in front of you while the person is talking would be an example of preparation.

2. *Paying Attention*—Concentrate on the speaker and what is being said. Don't interrupt with your own comments. Focus on the message and get the main points.

3. *Summarize*—Keep track of what is being said. Use key words and reduce the message into bite-sized chunks you'll be able to remember.

4. *Listen between Sentences*—Notice what's being said and how it is being said. Notice the gestures and expressions. This will help you understand what's being said and why.

5. *Ask Questions*—After you've heard the message, ask questions to make the meaning clearer. Your questions also give the speaker feedback so that he or she may make something clearer if necessary.

6. *Evaluate*—Once you've heard the message, seen the gestures, and clarified the meaning with your questions,

evaluate the information. Look for any personal prejudices (your feelings about the speaker or the subject, or
maybe you're just having a bad hair day) and make certain these prejudices haven't created any barriers to
your understanding.

The most difficult part of becoming a good listener is trying to put
your own thought processes aside to make way for the incoming message. Most people think at a rate of 1,000 to 2,000 words per minute,
but only talk at a rate of 100 to 200 words per minute.

Since we think a lot faster than we talk or other people talk, we
experience a big gap if we're a listener. Here's what happens: while
we're waiting to hear more, our own thinking begins to fill in the gap.
Sometimes, we're thinking about things that relate to what's being
discussed. Often, our thinking escapes to other subjects totally unre-
lated to the topic.

The Qualities of a Good Listener

Whatever listening skills you have now, there are a few easy steps to
take to become a better listener. These steps can be called "keys to
getting the message." And wherever you are in your listening skills, you
can always improve. Here's how.

1. *Maintain good eye contact.* Don't look around or read
or do something else. Focus on the speaker. Try this with
your significant other or your friends. You'll be surprised at
how much more they want to communicate with someone
who is totally focused on them and what they're saying.

2. *Give feedback.* Whether it's verbal or a gesture such as
a nod of the head.

3. *Listen between the lines.* Look for gestures, facial expressions, and all signs of another message along with
the words being used.

4. *Be patient.* Give the speaker time to finish before you
"jump" in with your two cents' worth.

5. ***Don't try to finish the speaker's sentences.*** This keeps you from listening well and it "butts in" on the message the speaker is trying to send.

6. ***Don't jump to conclusions.*** Try to be quiet until you get the "big picture."

7. ***Ask for clarification when you need it.*** Ask questions if you don't understand. You're not supposed to understand everything and it doesn't make you look stupid when you need to ask questions.

8. ***Keep an open mind.*** Just because this person doesn't work for your company or go to your church, he or she still has something to say. Don't let your own ideas—or your own prejudices—stand in your way of listening to the message.

9. ***Don't let distractions take you away from listening to the message.*** If you need to, turn off the radio, stop reading your paperwork, eating your meal, or whatever it is you're doing. Stop and focus on the speaker.

One More Word about Listening

Many times, the listening you as a professional driver will have to do comes in a situation when the speaker is not standing in front of you. Many times, the conversation comes over a pay phone or a cell phone, or you may read an e-mail or a written message. Because the conversation isn't face-to-face, your job as a listener becomes even more important. And you're working with a handicap because you may not be able to see the speaker's facial expression or gestures.

To bridge this barrier, it is your job to listen even more closely to the words, to ask questions when you don't totally understand, and even to repeat what the person said to make sure you've gotten the message. Here's a phone conversation we overheard between a driver and a shipper.

SHIPPER: We'll have that load ready at four this afternoon on the west dock of our East St. Louis location at the corner of Lockerby and Pine.

DRIVER: At the corner of Lockerby and Pine at 4 p.m. today on the west dock?

SHIPPER: That's right. Oh, and bring a dolly. We're running short on that dock.

DRIVER: I'll have a dolly on the west dock of Lockerby and Pine at 4 p.m. today.

It may sound like a waste of time to ask questions and repeat, but this gives the listener a chance to double-check information and to make any necessary notes. And, it gives the speaker a chance to make sure the listener has the right message, and it's also a chance to add something else (like "bring a dolly") to communicate the situation fully.

STEP TWO: THE SPOKEN WORD

Now that you're aware of the importance of your listening skills, it's important to look at the process of communicating your message. Here's what happens when you want to let someone else know your thoughts, wants, or needs.

1. You have something to say or you have an idea.

2. You determine to whom you need to speak.

3. You put your message or idea into words.

4. You use these words as you send the message to the receiver.

5. The listener receives your message, translates the meaning, and signals his or her understanding.

6. The listener sends feedback to you, letting you know he or she has received the message, and may respond with an answer, information, or a suggestion.

One of the most important steps in communicating your thoughts occurs when the listener translates the meaning of your words. This translation process is also called "perception." And what we know about perceptions is that they are never exactly the same. Here's an example of why they're not the same.

Joe drives for a refrigerated food fleet and has been forced to wait as long as eight hours at the warehouse dock of Big Giant Grocery Co. to unload. Bill drives for a different fleet and delivers to the same warehouse, yet he rarely has had to wait to unload.

Big Giant Grocery Co. gets taken over by another grocery chain and Joe and Bill meet in a truck stop restaurant shortly after the official announcement is made. "Well, that'll make for a good change," Bill tells Joe. "I bet you won't be having to wait eight hours at the dock anymore."

If you were Joe, would your perception of Bill's statement—that unloading times will improve with new management—be a positive one? The answer would probably be a big no because of Joe's bad experiences with the previous management.

Perceptions are usually formed out of personal experiences. These same perceptions often become barriers when we're sending and receiving messages. The important thing is to avoid these barriers to understanding.

Here's how you avoid barriers.

1. Don't let people's vocabulary, the way they dress, or their age keep you from hearing the message.

2. Don't make assumptions just because of the rig they drive.

3. Don't make assumptions based on poor grooming, lack of proper grammar, or poor organization.

4. Don't assume you know everything. Be open to new ideas and suggestions that could make your original idea even better.

A wise parent once told her children, "If you don't let people know what you want, you'll never get what you need."

Let's look at how you can get your messages across to others more effectively. To do that, you need to understand how attitudes change based on someone's individual needs. Psychologist Abraham Maslow developed a pyramid of individual needs and wants, showing how the focus of their desires changed as they moved through different levels. Understanding this pyramid helps you know how to communicate with others to be able to understand where they are on the scale of human values.

For example, you can't successfully speak to someone about making a donation to the United Way if he or she is at the bottom of the pyramid, still trying to get their basic needs met. And if someone is at the top of the pyramid, you probably won't be able to motivate that person with an awards program that includes a free steak dinner.

Look at the ads in today's magazines to see the various levels of needs at work. Ads for luxury cars and trucks appeal to the ego or status needs. Breath fresheners pinpoint social or acceptance needs. When you see an ad for burglar bars or fire alarms, these ads appeal to the security and safety needs.

A strong communicator will be able—with a few sentences—to find out where the other person is on Maslow's pyramid of human needs. If a person needs to be accepted in the group, he or she will respond when your message makes that person feel a part. If they're still working at the safety and security level, reassuring them that they're doing a good job will make them feel more secure. And if they're working on the basic needs level, offering them a free lunch or presenting them with a new uniform will get the message across every time.

In business, the effectiveness of how someone communicates is measured in two ways.

1. Whether the listener provides the information asked for or follows the suggested behavior.

2. Whether the result is worth the cost and effort necessary for the communication.

When the shipper told the driver when the load would be ready, where to find it, and to bring a dolly, the effectiveness of the communication was measured if the driver was on time and at the right place with the dolly.

As you work through your route of pickups and deliveries, or when you deliver a shipment and then load the next one, check yourself. Are you communicating clearly? Do you understand what someone is saying or asking? And if you don't understand, are you asking questions to help the speaker make the message clearer?

It may take a little more time, but making sure that you're communicating effectively will make your job easier and will make your day better. Guaranteed!

Chapter 3

Customer Service: It's Part of the Job

Trucking is a competitive business. In today's market, large and small companies emphasize customer service as the difference between themselves and their competitor down the street.

Many trucking terminals look the same and fleets are about the same age. The rates carriers charge are about the same, and it takes most companies the same amount of time to move a shipment from point A to point B.

So why does ABC Computer Co. choose one carrier over another?

In most cases, the difference comes down to how that shipper is treated by its carrier of choice. When the shipper calls in for a pickup, is the dispatcher friendly? Does he listen? Does he act unhurried? Are special instructions followed?

And when the pickup is made, is the driver well groomed? Is the driver professional and efficient? And is the driver pleasant while he or she is completing the paperwork for the shipment?

All of these aspects of the contact a customer has with your company could be classified as customer service, and today, companies who succeed are not those who just provide good customer service but extraordinary service!

A few years ago, some of this country's more successful business owners came up with the phrase, "Extraordinary Customer Service," meaning "always going the extra mile for the customer." Is this something your company does as a carrier? Is it something you do for every customer?

You may not think of it in this way, but providing extraordinary customer service can help you gain more satisfaction from your job. It can also help build a reputation for your firm, as it encourages others to remember that extraordinary customer service can mean the difference between a successful firm and one that's barely able to break even at the end of the month.

Or look at this way. Extraordinary customer service can expand business opportunities in any market; lack of good customer service can drive any business down the drain. Take your pick.

So why is great customer service so important? Because we have become a service-oriented society. We expect good customer service everywhere we go. And customer service is everywhere. Just take a look around you. At the grocery store, most checkers are trained to greet the customer, smile, and begin checking out the order as soon as possible. Scanners have taken the place of the checker hand-keying the prices on every item. That makes the process faster and, supposedly, less open to mistakes. Why? Because customers complained that checking out took too much time and too many errors were made. So as soon as electronic scanners were available and affordable, almost all stores had them installed.

Wal-Mart has greeters at almost all of their stores and is known for its excellent policy on returned items. Home Depot has experienced home repair people on staff to answer the questions of do-it-yourselfers who come in to buy home repair items. Albertson's stores have a 100 percent guaranteed grocery carry-out policy, with no tipping expected or allowed.

Most large stores now offer motorized carts for customers with disabilities, and many of these same stores advertise in-store shopping assistance for these customers and for elderly shoppers.

How often have you been in a store, waiting for someone to help you? When no clerk appeared, you probably felt your blood pressure rising, and when you had to search to find someone to take your money, you probably mumbled something about this being your last time at that store.

WHAT IS EXTRAORDINARY CUSTOMER SERVICE?

Customer service is really a simple concept. It means that a company— or individual workers—meet a customer's needs so that the customer feels special and, more important, feels that your company cares about all of his or her needs. Providing good customer service means the customer will remember your company and will want to do business with your firm again.

The difference between a company offering so-so customer service and one that offers great customer service is the commitment of every person on the staff to go the extra mile to meet every customer's needs. That's right. Every person.

In the transportation industry, that means the shop is committed to keeping the equipment in good shape so that there are no delays, and city pickup and delivery drivers can be there when the shipment's ready to move off the customer's dock.

It means the dispatcher is cordial, efficient, and able to provide a truck when the customer is ready for it. It also means the dispatcher has a good relationship with his or her drivers so those drivers will arrive on time, take good care of the shipment and paperwork, and bring it back to the dock so the freight can get on the road on time.

It means the drivers are professional, courteous, efficient, and caring about the job they do. It means management is committed to extraordinary customer service and are willing to recognize on-time work, professional treatment of their customers, and will reward drivers who consistently go the extra mile for their customers.

Bottom line: customer service is the responsibility of everyone on the payroll; those who are part-time as well as those who manage the company.

Four little words should be at the heart of everything your company does for each of its customers: MAKE ME FEEL IMPORTANT (MMFI). Here's an example.

A customer calls your dispatcher for a pickup. The dispatcher takes the information and thanks the customer for the call. The driver is at the customer's dock when the customer indicated the shipment would be ready. There's no waiting. The trailer is loaded efficiently and properly. The driver is friendly and professional, and treats everyone on the dock—from the foreman to the dock hands—with cordial respect. He or she takes the paperwork, signs any documents necessary, and the load is on its way. It arrives at the consignee's dock when promised, on schedule, and in good shape.

Once the shipment is delivered, the paperwork is completed, the shipper is billed, and pays the bill, feeling that they've gotten good value from your company. And everyone along the way was willing to go the extra mile and was pleasant to work with.

That makes the shipper feel important. It also prompts the shipper to pick up the phone and call your company when they have another load for the lanes you serve.

So, how do you make each customer feel important?

First of all, you need to know your customers. These include people who work on every level of the firms you serve, from the part-time clean-up personnel to the dispatcher, the dock foreman, the billing agent, the receptionist, the sales force, and the management.

One company that was losing business investigated why their customers were suddenly calling other carriers. What they found was when a customer called—whether it was for a pickup or for clarification on a bill—the customers were made to feel like they were interrupting the person at the other end of the line.

Management immediately began to make changes so that when customers called, they were treated in a professional manner and their requests were handled in a timely fashion. "If people didn't need some type of service from you, you wouldn't have jobs," the company's manager explained to his staff.

DEALING WITH ALL TYPES OF CUSTOMERS

Customers come in all types and all flavors. Serving the general public isn't always easy because this means you are dealing with a cross-section of humanity. Each individual is different. Each comes with different experiences and different attitudes. Each also comes with a whole new set of opinions and problems.

When you are dealing with customers, it is important to understand something about the different types of personalities and what may be needed to work successfully with each type.

For example, you may be confronted by a typical **Type A personality**. These people are very busy, very driven, and very confident. They are loud in groups and traditionally like to dominate the conversation. They know what they want and they usually want it now!

When you deal with Type As, you must be strong. They do not care for weak people. Stay on task, ask only the questions you need answered, and be specific. Provide them choices when possible and stay out of their way, but be ready to help whenever humanly possible.

Type B personalities are happy-go-lucky people. They want to be accepted and liked by everyone. With Type B people, you should be open and friendly. Happy-go-lucky people enjoy conversation and like to do most of the talking. Let them talk about their lives. Let them tell you about their families and let them verbalize their specific needs. If you have an opportunity, provide them with stories about how certain services have been used successfully. Try not to push or rush these people, however. Listen as much as possible and be patient. Your patience and hard work will pay off.

Type C personalities are your cautious customers. They need to be treated informally and they need to trust you, so take your time getting to know them, providing them with reassurance and guidance every step of the way. Don't rush them to make decisions. Give them time to think. These customers are more satisfied when they come to a decision in a calm and unhurried environment.

Finally, there are the **Type R personalities**. These are people of order who know all the rules and expect you to follow them. They know exactly what customer service is and how you should act. Know your facts—and your business—and present yourself in such a way that will meet their specific needs. Let them know exactly what you can do and when you will be able to do it.

FIRST IMPRESSIONS ARE USUALLY REMEMBERED

When ABC Carriers first called on CDE Shippers, the office manager noticed that the driver's uniform was stained and dingy. When they called for a pickup, the dispatcher gave them an estimated time of arrival (ETA) for the driver at their dock, and that driver was an hour late. The dock supervisor reported the trailer was filthy and the equipment, shoddy.

Was CDE's first impression of ABC a lasting one? Unfortunately, yes. After trying to do business with time-sensitive shipments on a few occasions, CDE was forced to call another carrier.

First impressions are usually lasting and first impressions are also usually correct. Oftentimes, these first impressions are the only ones you're allowed to make, so they should be representative of the firm you work for and they should be positive impressions of yourself.

A positive first impression is one that creates confidence in the mind of your customer. Here are a few tips to make a good first impression.

 Let the customer know you are capable of handling this or any other situation.

 Call your customers by name, not just when you meet and greet them, but anytime you see them, and several times during the conversation.

Let customers know you are interested in what they're saying by stopping what you are doing, making eye contact, and truly listening.

Do what you say you're going to do. You want your customer to think of you as a person who is helpful, knowledgeable, and one who keeps his or her word.

Provide answers to any questions your customers might have, and if you don't know the answers, make a phone call on the spot and get them the answer they need to do business with you and your company.

Be resourceful. Make suggestions when asked.

Create confidence in simple ways. Smile, make eye contact, shake hands, use the customer's name, and remember to always to thank them for their business.

Always be ready to go the extra mile and, when possible, provide extras your customer may not expect.

STATEMENTS YOU MAKE IN THE WAY YOU DRESS

First impressions are based on your conduct and your appearance. Truck drivers often complain about the way they are treated by shippers and receivers. But how you present yourself to these customers will have a large bearing on how they will treat you. Gaining their respect begins with the way you dress.

Some trucking companies choose to issue drivers a uniform and expect drivers to wear them to project a professional image. Even if you are not required to wear a uniform, there are a number of ways you can be professional in the way you dress.

 Keep clean. Wash your clothes regularly. Grease and sweat stains are not particularly appealing.

Keep tidy. Tuck your shirt in. Don't wear clothes with holes. Keep your boots polished or your shoes clean.

 Stay on top of personal hygiene. If you are running hard, it can be tough to take care of your teeth, hair, and the like. But if you let go too much in this area, you won't make a lot of friends.

Dress sensibly. T-shirts with offensive statements may be good for a laugh with your friends, but your customers may not see the humor.

If you follow these general guidelines, you can still be creative in the way you dress and express your individuality. Remember, if you're going to make a statement, make it a positive one, not a negative one.

WHY LISTENING IS THE NUMBER ONE PRIORITY IN COMMUNICATING

For many people, listening is a very difficult task. To listen well, you must have your ears open and your mouth shut. Remember, listening is different from hearing. Listening means you understand what the person is saying to you. Hearing is simply the physical act of sound going into your ears. Only when you comprehend what your customer is saying are you truly listening.

Never "pretend" to listen because your customer will instantly know you are not listening. More importantly, if you're faking, you probably won't clearly hear or understand their problem or request.

When speaking—and listening—to your customer, be aware of your posture and your gestures. Clients will know you are not completely interested in what they are saying if you stand with your arms crossed over your chest, you don't make eye contact, or you heave a heavy sigh.

The bottom line is, treat your customer like you would treat the CEO of your company, and make sure you give each person you work with the same amount of attention and respect.

DEALING WITH THE ANGRY CUSTOMER

It would be great if all your customers were pleasant and rational, but as you well know, life isn't like that. Once or twice a week, you'll run into the customer who just isn't a happy camper. And you're not to blame.

He may have had a spat with his partner before he left for work that morning, or he may have just received a call from school, telling him that his son or daughter had been tardy to class every day this week. Or his spouse may have called to let him know the electricity had just been turned off because SOMEBODY had forgotten to pay last month's electric bill.

Whatever the reason, human beings can't be expected to be happy all the time. When you're dealing with unhappy customers, keep your own emotions in control and don't escalate the situation. Never try to "out smart-mouth" or "out nasty" a customer. And don't take the customer's anger personally. Let the customer vent if that's what he or she wants to do. Then you move on to the facts so you can solve the problem, if the problem involves something you or your company have done.

Acknowledge that the customer is not happy with the situation. Then tell him or her you are sorry for the trouble and that the frustration is understandable. Let the customer know you want to help.

Finally, tell the customer what you plan to do to solve the problem. Most of the time, this will include contacting someone at the company who can take over from there. But, most important of all, do what you say you're going to do and then follow up with the customer. You may be the only person from your company that he or she deals with on a day-to-day basis.

Whatever you do, never use a negative or quote a company policy. People don't want to hear what you *can't* do. They want to know what you *can* do to solve their problem.

It is much better to use phrases like, "This is what I *can* do...." or "Let's see what we *can* do about this" or "I haven't heard of this problem before. Can you give me more details?"

By maintaining a positive attitude, you are a creating an environment in which you can help this customer solve his or her problem, or at least provide this unhappy customer with some satisfaction.

Steve Leonard, a customer service guru, once said this about extraordinary customer service:

Rule One: The customer is always right.

Rule Two: If the customer is wrong, see rule number one.

Here are some easy-to-remember steps in handling customer complaints. These not only will help build customer loyalty, but also will open the door for feedback and help you continually improve the service you are providing every customer. These are called the Six Steps to T.H.A.N.K.S.:

Thank your customer for bringing the problem to your attention.

Hear the problem and listen carefully.

Apologize for the inconvenience the customer has experienced.

Need more information? Ask!

Know the solution and be prepared to offer it.

Solve the problem or find someone who can.

SOME FINAL COMMENTS

To provide extraordinary customer service, you need to listen, to offer options, to find solutions, to do what you say you're going to do, to follow up when there's a problem, to make certain the customer is satisfied, and to be willing to go the extra mile every day of the week.

How do you provide extraordinary customer service 100 percent of the time? Just follow these steps.

1. Know your customer and fully understand your customer's needs.

2. When you ask questions, listen closely and carefully.

3. When there's a problem, keep your cool and listen. Then offer solutions.

4. MMFI—make every customer feel important.

5. Be patient. Dealing with difficult people takes practice.

6. Be responsive to each new problem a customer wants you to solve.

7. Be respectful and pleasant to everyone you deal with at the customer location. And do the same at your own dock or office.

8. Each day, commit yourself to making a difference at every stop and every customer location.

9. Make an effort to go the extra mile in every situation, no matter how large or small.

10. Decide how good your service really is. Is it the kind of service you would expect for yourself? If you've delivered the kind of service you would appreciate, you've done a good job!

SERVICE WITH A SMILE AND AN EXTRA MILE

When Lily Samson ordered her grandson's bike, she wasn't sure how she would handle it once it was shipped from the manufacturer, but she decided she would worry about that when it got there.

You see, Lily—a sprightly 70-year-old—had been plagued with arthritis for several years. Her hands were deformed with the disease, and with the lack of use of her hands, her arms had become quite week.

The bicycle—designed so that her grandson with cerebral palsy would be able to ride with the help of his younger brother—weighed more than 200 pounds. Lily didn't know how she would handle such a big crate.

But like so many of us, Lily discovered a guardian angel in the form of Joe Lemmings, a driver for one of the local carriers.

"Mrs. Samson," said the friendly voice over the telephone, "my name is Joe Lemmings. I'm with ABC Carriers and I have a delivery here for you. Will you be home tomorrow between 12 noon and 2 p.m.?"

"Is it my grandson's bicycle?" she asked.

"Yes. Yes, it is, a crate from Worksman's Cycles in New York."

"Well, yes. I'll be here tomorrow, but I don't know if I can help you get that thing into my garage."

"Don't worry, 'ma'am. We'll figure out something," the driver reassured her.

The next day, Joe pulled his truck up to the curb outside Lily's house. It was exactly 12:30 p.m.

It took her several moments to answer the door, but when she opened it, she found a sturdy young man in a crisp uniform. "Mrs. Samson? I'm Joe Lemmings. Now, where do you want me to put this big box?"

"Just inside the garage would be good," she smiled, trying to make his job as easy as possible.

She followed him to the curb and waited while he lowered the crate with the truck's tailgate.

Propping the crate onto a dolly, he rolled it down the driveway while she went in to open the garage door.

"So, what have we got here?" Lemmings asked.

"It's a special bike for my grandson. He has cerebral palsy and can't ride bikes like the other kids," she explained. "I found out about this one from his therapist and thought I would surprise him with it for his birthday next week."

The wooden crate was as large as a small freezer. "Why don't you give me a minute to check in with my dispatcher and I'll help you open the crate," the driver offered.

A few minutes later he was back with some tools to pry the top and sides from the crate.

Sure enough, inside was a bright and shiny bike. But, with one problem. The wheels were not attached.

"Oh my," said the woman. "I didn't know it would have to be assembled."

"No problem," the driver said. "We can get this taken care of in a minute or two." He pulled the instructions from a pouch inside the crate and started reading. And within five minutes, he had attached one of the wheels and was ready to start on the other.

"Oh, I just hate to be so much bother," the woman apologized.

The driver didn't stop his work until both wheels were attached and the bike was ready to ride. "No trouble at all. Glad to do it," he said.

Lily invited him in for a glass of tea, but the driver needed to get back to his deliveries. He still had a full afternoon ahead of him. "At least let me go get you a cold drink to take along," she offered.

"Sounds great," Joe replied. "I could use a Coke about now."

Later that year, thanks to several letters written by satisfied customers—including Lily Samson—Joe won the company's service award, a plaque, an additional day off, and a $100 bill.

During the banquet, as Joe accepted the award, he didn't stop to name the times he had gone the extra mile to help a customer. Instead, he shared with those attending how good it felt every time he could make a difference, whether it was getting a big corporation's shipment delivered on time or helping a grandmother unload her grandson's bike. "It's a feeling I can't describe," Joe concluded. "But, when you feel it, you'll know it. And you won't forget it."

Chapter 4

Sharing the Road

If you're having a tough time dealing with traffic and you're holding out hope that congestion will ease, we have some bad news. The number of cars and trucks on the road is expected to continue to grow over the next few decades, outpacing the ability of states to build highways and roads to accommodate them all.

Your best strategy for coping and easing your stress levels is to get better at sharing the road. That means, first of all, exemplary driving on your part and practicing common courtesy. Maintain safe following distances, stay in your own lane when you aren't passing, signal when you do need to pass or turn, and don't block other traffic by driving alongside another slow-moving vehicle.

Newer trucks give you more technology and better engineered equipment such as improved mirrors, blind-spot detectors, and better visibility to see and be aware of the vehicles around you. The convex mirror on the right side of your truck can be your friend. Learn to use it and other viewing aids so that it becomes second nature.

While these viewing tools are helpful, your most important aids are the two A's: Attitude and Anticipation. It's been said the true definition of a professional driver is someone who conducts himself in a safe manner to make up for the mistakes of others. That's the model attitude. You should always expect that someone else is going to mess up and not see you, or barge into a space in front of you, or sit in your blind spot for miles on end.

Anticipation plays a big part in space management. You need to be constantly looking ahead and to the side, and expecting erratic behavior from other motorists. Don't get caught up in duels with another motorist for a space. Back off and try to maintain safe following distances.

Finally, don't get distracted. More accidents are being caused by drivers busy with cellular phones, computers, or entertainment systems. Stay focused on the road, particularly when you are driving in traffic. A moment's inattention can cause a fatal collision. Always remember, an 80,000-pound rig that is out of control can be a lethal weapon.

WISE USE OF THE CB RADIO

The CB radio was adopted by truckers as a communication tool a number of decades ago. Over time, it has helped truckers get out of jams, both of their own doing and by occurrences out of their own control. It has acted as a valuable lifeline, and has saved many lives when truckers and other motorists have been caught in blizzards or driving in blinding fog.

While new forms of wireless communication such as cellular phones, pagers, and satellite tracking systems have made the CB obsolete for many applications, it is still a cheap, handy tool for short-range communication.

The CB, by its nature, is a public medium. Anyone can listen and participate in conversations. That's great for free speech, but it also makes it open to abuse. Anyone with a grudge, a cross to bear, misdirected anger, or a generally vindictive nature can hide behind a CB microphone and use it to trash talk others.

Using the CB to voice your intolerance does little to boost your self-esteem. It also does a lot to damage the image of truckers. Families driving by in their cars may already have reason to dislike truckers before they listen in on the CB. Spewing hate-filled diatribes or engaging in lewdness only confirms and reinforces their thoughts.

To boost your self-esteem and the image of the industry, keep your conversations on the CB free of inappropriate language. Try to build others up instead of tearing them down. The CB can be a wonderful medium for conducting long, thoughtful conversations, or telling stories on those long, lonely nights at the wheel. But if you are experiencing stress on the road, resist the temptation to vent your frustration on the CB. Instead, take a deep breath and wait until your mood changes. The CB is a powerful tool. Use it wisely.

Chapter 5

Training on the Move

For most Americans, getting enough training to land a job becomes a high priority somewhere between the high school diploma/GED and landing that first job that actually pays the bills. However, as the 21st century dawned on this planet, many of these same folks had decided that more skills were needed if they were going to keep pace with technology and job demands.

How they could accomplish these goals? Through distance education.

Buckminster Fuller, an architect, engineer, designer, teacher, author, inventor, and a respected visionary, had this to say about life in the new millennium:

> *"Education is going to be number one among the great world industries" (Thorvaldsen, 1980, p. 3).*

As the realities of the new century began to emerge in the late 1990s, it was abundantly clear that education would be ongoing, and that many people would learn two, three, or four career skill sets in a lifetime. It was also clear that evolving technology would create an ongoing need for lifelong learning.

But who has time to quit work and return to the classroom to learn new skills or new careers? Obviously, it is not practical for most people to quit work. It is even more impractical to suggest that we would be able to quit work and go back to school three or four times in our lifetime.

Enter distance education: one solution to roadblocks that sometimes accompany lifetime learning.

Distance education is nothing new. In fact, centuries ago, wanderers would bring information from one point on the map to another, sharing their knowledge through word-of-mouth, street-corner professors of sorts.

By the middle 1800s, printed materials were used to take learning beyond the walls of colleges and universities. By the 1930s, radios were broadcasting distance learning to mass audiences. Today's distance learning is rooted in early correspondence courses offered by universities and through extension programs designed to educate students using a paper-based method.

Public television brought learning into the homes of hundreds of families. In the 1960s, for example, the Dallas Public Television Station began offering driver education programs to area high schoolers before they took the driving test, and later, Dallas County Community College offered many of its basic education courses in English, math, and history through public television broadcasts.

In 1969, the British Open University began providing international learning opportunities and became more visible as the Internet began to take shape. By the early 1990s, more than 50,000 students from around the world were taking courses offered by the BOU.

Part of the British Open University's growth can be attributed to the fact that they broadcast video versions of many of the University's courses on the British Broadcasting Company's channel each week. At a seminar in the early 1990s, one speaker noted that with the help of the Internet, he was able to teach one course to students in five countries, and while called away to present a paper, he had actually taught the course from his hotel room. When asked how many students could be taught by one professor offering one course, his response was, "Thousands."

WHAT THIS MEANS TO PROFESSIONAL DRIVERS

It is no secret that many professional drivers today fill their hours on the road with audiotapes or books on tape. In many cases, this same time and these same tape players could be used to learn something new by listening to course lectures offered by schools that teach distance learning classes.

Add a laptop computer and you're ready for online learning that may apply to a certificate of specialization in a certain area, to completing courses to meet degree requirements, or just to provide information you've always been interested in knowing.

Stephen Levey, executive director of distance education for Houston Community College System, says most community colleges today offer many courses through distance education. And many colleges and universities offer full degrees through distance learning. According to Levey, distance learning has become extremely popular over the past five years due to wider availability of improved technology. Key developments have been the evolution of the Internet, and the ability of computers to store large amounts of information and retrieve this information through CD-ROMs or DVDs.

Some courses are offered over the Internet at no charge. Most colleges and universities, however, usually charge tuition and fees for each course. Many times, the textbooks may be purchased online through amazon.com or BN.com (Barnes & Noble Bookstores).

At Houston Community College, most courses offer three semester hours of credit. The cost of a three-semester hour course for in-district students taking distance learning is $117. For those living outside the state of Texas, the cost is $369 for a three-semester hour course. The largest distance education enrollments are in the basic academic courses like English, history, math, philosophy, and psychology.

In the area of workforce education, popular courses include those found under the headings of accounting, business administration, computer science/technology, chemical technology, law enforcement, fire protection, real estate, and technical communication such as Web page design or Internet Web page development.

Many of these courses do not require anything more than signing up. Some use the Internet and accept credit cards, then require buying the book and beginning study on the first module.

If you decide to take a course for credit, a community college or university near your home is a good starting place, so you can get face-to-face information as well as information from their Web site.

And, if you decide to take courses toward a degree, be prepared to produce your high school transcript, and those from any college or university you've attended in the past. If you want to take the course and don't want the credit, the sign-up process may be a bit different. You may not need transcripts but simply a Social Security card and the tuition and fees, if any are charged.

Some distance courses are offered through a series of videos you can check out and then return. Others broadcast course lectures through a local public education channel or cable channel. Still others are totally online, and that includes any reading materials, too.

If you begin a course at a college or university and then find you will need more than a semester to complete it, you can always apply for an extension. Usually—with free courses—you can take as long as you wish to complete a course.

You may want to check with a Professional Truck Driving Institute (PTDI) certified school if you are interested in taking a trucking-related course. Schools with PTDI-certified courses are listed by state on the PTDI Web site at http://www.ptdi.org. Not all of these schools offer distance learning, but some may have courses available.

EXAMPLES OF COURSES AVAILABLE OVER THE WORLD WIDE WEB

Barnes & Noble University

Barnes & Noble University (found at www.barnesandnobleuniversity.com) offers 50 free online courses each month. Each course is taught by an expert in the field. The courses offered cover everything from technology and computer skills to literature, business, and other topics.

Teachers communicate with students and students talk to each other through the Barnes & Noble message boards. All of the courses use textbooks in conjunction with the lesson.

Once you decide to take a course, a syllabus and lessons are available online. And you can even take notes online.

A sampling of courses include:

The Bible as Literature	All Aboard: Railroad in American History
The Lord of the Rings	Martin Luther King: His Life and Legacy
Writing for Children	The Civil War Era
Alfred Hitchcock: Genius at Work	Learn to Play the Guitar
Basic Dog Training	Picasso, Braque, and Dawn of Cubism
Choosing a Home Computer	Designing Your Own Garden
Exploring Herbal Medicine	Introduction to Wine
Yoga for Novices	401k Basics by Bloomberg
Getting Things Done	Financial Planning
Introduction to Chess	Responsible Credit Card Spending
Online Investing	Managing Your Debt
Introduction to Microsoft Visual Basic	Introduction to Perl
Intro to Astronomy	Introduction to Cosmetology
Tax Basics (2002 Edition)	Plan Your Estate
Choosing the Right Diet	Stress, Sanity, and Survival
Total Memory Workshop	Great Home Videos: Shoot Like a Pro

Free-Ed.Net

At http://www.free-ed.net, you can take courses ranging from general education to information technology, and from introduction to human anatomy to mastering C++ and Photography 110—Elements of Modern Photography.

If you're interested in health care, the medical terminology course may be for you, and if you're musically inclined, the fundamentals of music course may be interesting. There is no charge for Free-Ed courses and you don't have to sign up. Just find a course that suits your needs and get started! All courses are conducted online. Free-Ed.Net will be opening new classes and adding new courses through 2005. For high school teachers, courses will be available for brush-up to meet new requirements. The list of high school subjects will be complete in 2005

Free-Ed is not intended to replace formal education, but provides a review of material you've previously learned, extends your vocational skills, and expands your understanding of material related to your work, hobby, or special interest.

Sample courses include:

Accounting	Journalism
Art	Hospitality
Automotive Technology	Computer Languages
Bookkeeping	Astronomy
English	Manufacturing Technology
Construction Technology	GED Preparation
Business	Biology
English as Second Language	Welding Technology
Electronics Technology	GMAT Preparation
Economics	Chemistry

HVAC

Performing Arts

Computer Info Systems

Computer Technology

Literature

GRE Preparation

Environmental Technology

Geography

Finance

Technical Writing

Modern Languages

Photography

Fashion & Textiles

Earth Sciences

Marketing

Human Ecology

Classical Languages

Anatomy and Physiology

Health Occupations

Physics

Personal Finance

Sociology

QuicKnowledge.com

These distance learning courses come with a price tag, although they're very affordable—beginning at $9.95 per course—or you can pay an annual fee, depending on your needs and your goals.

This site—located at www.quicknowledge.com—divides its course offerings into two groups: a business category and a personal category. You can register online and take a course by computer, using a credit card to pay for the course. Each course offers a way to evaluate what you've learned and extra materials to help you understand each topic clearly.

A sampling of course topics under the Business category includes:

Achieving Personal Goals

Telephone Sales Skills

Basics of Effective Communication

Time Management

Basics of Effective Selling

Avoiding Burnout

Building Strong Customer Relationships	Understanding Contracts
Dealing with Difficult Customers	Managing Change

Courses listed under the Personal category include:

Conflict Intervention

Guardianship Decisions for Elderly Loved Ones

Internet Basics

Managing Stress

Managing Your 401k

Personal Financial Planning

Recognizing and Managing Anger

Like any other activity, distance learning may not be for everyone. But for many, distance learning provides opportunities that were not available 10 or 15 years ago. For someone working full time, distance learning offers a chance to expand understanding and broaden horizons during free time. For others, distance learning provides an opportunity to learn, no matter where they are.

Distance learning requires an investment in a computer with a modem and access to the Internet. Courses, however, can cost as little as nothing or, in some cases, several hundred dollars.

The value of distance learning, however, depends on you, the learner. It can be an opportunity or it can be a pain in the neck. It can be something to pass the time or it can be a waste of time. It's up to you to decide.

Chapter 6

Eating Right: The Key to Your Health

It's normal for most Americans to gain weight as they get older. At age 40, most would have a tough time getting into the jeans they wore in high school.

But for the professional truck driver, the risk of excessive weight gain is much higher due to poor eating habits, lack of exercise, and stress.

Being overweight is a well-established risk factor for such diseases as stroke, heart disease, high blood pressure, diabetes, and cancer. It also makes conditions like arthritis and back pain worse.

The following are a few indications that truck drivers have a problem controlling their weight.

A 1993 study of 2,945 truck drivers attending a trade show noted that 73 percent were "heavy."

A 1993 study examining the prevalence of sleep apnea in 125 drivers for one company revealed that 71 percent of the drivers were classified as "heavy."

A 1994 study revealed that "heavy" drivers had a two-fold higher accident involvement rate than non-"heavy" drivers.

A 2001 study at several truck stops in the midwest and southwest revealed that 60 percent of the drivers were "heavy."

Many drivers can find themselves on a slippery downhill slide toward ending a good job and becoming a safety hazard to themselves and others. It is easy to get into an endless cycle of unhealthy eating and inadequate exercise.

You can get out of this cycle by eating right. Food is fuel for the body. If you attempt to put more fuel in your truck than it can hold, the excess would run out onto the ground. When you eat more food than your body can use, it turns into fat that is stored. To prevent this storage of fat, you have to burn more fuel than you put in.

Let's look at the basics of nutrition. The fuel you put in your body is measured in calories. Most food contains protein, carbohydrates, fat, fiber, vitamins, and minerals. You should know how many calories your body uses in a day. A simple way to calculate this is to multiply your body weight by 10 and then add 20 percent to that number. So if you weighed 200 pounds, it would be:

200 pounds x 10 = 2,000.

20% x 2,000 = 400.

2,000 + 400 = 2,400 total calories needed per day to maintain your current weight.

Now let's look at the calorie content in a typical day for many truckers.

Breakfast: A two-egg omelet, three strips of bacon, cup of hash browns, one slice of toast with two pats of butter or margarine, glass of fruit juice, and coffee.   **685 calories**

Lunch: A quarter-pound cheeseburger, large fries, and a 16-ounce soda.   **1,166 calories**

Dinner: Fried chicken, two pieces (breast and wing), biscuit, mashed potatoes and gravy, corn on the cob, and a 16-ounce soda.   **1,232 calories**

Snacks: Two doughnuts (300 calories each); one four-ounce bag of potato chips (150 calories per ounce)   **1,200 calories**

Let's add it all up:

685 calories for breakfast

1,166 calories for lunch

1,232 calories for dinner

1,200 calories for snack

4,083 calories for the day

If you weighed 200 pounds and you ate like this every day, it's highly unlikely that you'll stay 200 pounds for long. Another nutritional fact: one pound of body fat equals about 3,500 calories. Therefore, losing a pound requires a 3,500-calorie deficit. Also, consuming 3,500 more calories than the body needs will result in a one-pound gain of fat.

To reduce the amount of fuel you put into your body, you have to make better choices about what you eat. Since fat contains more than twice the calories of carbohydrates and protein, the most effective thing you can do is reduce the amount of fat in your diet. The best strategy is to cut out fried foods. Fried foods contain many more calories than broiled or baked. That means no fried chicken, no fried hamburgers, and no more of the number-one choice of truck drivers everywhere: chicken fried steak.

The greatest amount of fat comes directly from fats and oils as well as salad dressings, candy, gravies, sauces, potato chips, and pastries such as doughnuts.

Depending on food choices, meat, poultry, fish, and eggs may account for the next largest amount of fat in an average diet, followed by milk, cheese, yogurt, and frozen desserts like ice cream.

Fruits, vegetables, and grains don't supply much fat. With a few exceptions, these foods are high in fat only if fat is added during food preparation or processing, for example, in French fries.

The best solution is to balance the food you eat with physical activity to maintain or reduce your weight. Most Americans gain weight over a period of years. To reduce that weight gain, eat less and exercise more. Choose a diet with plenty of grain products, vegetables, and fruits. Grain products, vegetables, and fruits are excellent sources of many nutrients as well as fiber.

Eat a variety of foods. Each day, your body needs the nutrients that a variety of foods supply. Most foods have a variety of nutrients, but no food has all of them.

Go easy on salt and sodium. Many individuals have blood pressure that is sensitive to sodium. For these people, a high-sodium intake along with obesity, heredity, and getting older, contributes to high blood pressure.

When your throat feels dry or when you are sweating, you probably reach for the water bottle. Is that often enough? Do you get enough water if you only drink when you are thirsty? Probably not.

Your body is about 70 percent water, depending on your age. Body tissues of all types contain water,-some more than others. Blood is about 83 percent water. Muscle tissue is about 73 percent water. Even bones contain about 20 percent water. Nearly every function of your body needs water. Water regulates your body temperature, transports nutrients and oxygen to your body cells, and carries away waste products. It has many other functions, and is the main part of every body fluid including blood, gastric juice, and urine. It also softens the stool to help prevent constipation.

Most persons need about 8 to 12 cups of water per day. Sometimes you may need more. The following factors may increase your water needs:

 exposure to extreme heat or cold

strenuous work or exercise

exposure to heated or recirculated air for long periods of time, such as driving for long periods of time in an air-conditioned truck

 illness, because fever, diarrhea, and vomiting all cause increased loss of water

The best way to get enough water is to take water with you in your truck. Most small bottles of water contain about two cups. To get your

needed 8 to 12 cups of water, you will have to drink about four to six bottles per day. Fluids that you drink with your meals count toward your 8 to 12 cups per day; so any fluids consumed with your meals can be subtracted from the 8 to 12 cups.

The Food Guide Pyramid

More specific information on what foods to eat is described in the Food Guide Pyramid developed by the U.S. Department of Agriculture in the late 1990s.

HOW MANY SERVINGS

The chart below tells how many servings are needed, depending on gender, age, and activity level

	Less Active Women, Older Adults	Active Women, Less Active Men	Active Men
Calories	about	about	about
Per day	1,600	2,200	2,800
Bread Group	6	9	11
Vegetable Group	3	4	5
Fruit Group	2	3	4
Milk Group	2–3	2–3	2–3
Meat Group	2, for a total of 5 ounces	2, for a total of 6 ounces	3, for a total of 7 ounces

From Shaw, A., Fulton, L., Davis, C., & Hogbin, M. Using the food guide pyramid: A resource for nutrition educators. Washington, DC: U.S. Department of Agriculture Center for Nutrition Policy and Promotion (CNPP).

Serving Sizes for Food Groups

A bread, cereal, rice, and pasta group serving is:

One slice enriched or whole-grain bread (one ounce)

One-half a hamburger roll, bagel, pita bread, or English muffin

One (six-inch) tortilla

One-half cup cooked rice or pasta

One-half cup cooked oatmeal, grits, cream of wheat, or any other whole grains

One ounce ready-to-eat cereal

Three to four small crackers

One (four-inch diameter) pancake or waffle

Two medium cookies

(One-half cup of pasta or rice is about the size of a small fist)

A vegetable group serving is:

One-half cup chopped raw, nonleafy vegetables

One cup of leafy raw vegetables such as lettuce, spinach, or cabbage

One-half cup cooked vegetables

One-half cup cooked beans, peas, or lentils

One small baked potato (three ounces)

Three-fourths cup of vegetable juice

(One-half cup of vegetables is about the size of a small fist)

(One cup of chopped fresh vegetables is about the size of a small hand holding a tennis ball)

A fruit group serving is:

One medium piece of fruit (apple, orange, banana, or peach)

One-half grapefruit, mango, or papaya

Three-fourths cup of juice

One-half cup of canned, frozen, or cooked fruit

One-fourth cup of dried fruit

One-half cup berries or cut up fruit

(One-half cup of fruit is about the size of a small fist)

A milk, yogurt, and cheese group serving is:

One cup of milk or buttermilk

One cup yogurt

One and one-half ounces of cheese

(a one-ounce piece of cheese is the size of your thumb)

A meat, poultry, fish, dry beans, eggs, and nut group serving is:

Three ounces of cooked lean meat, poultry, or fish

Three ounces lean sliced deli meat (turkey, ham, or beef)

Three ounces canned tuna or salmon packed in water

Two eggs (if fried or scrambled, fat content is increased; best if boiled or poached)

One-half cup egg substitute

Four tablespoons of peanut butter

One-half cup of nuts

Four ounces of tofu

One small chicken leg or thigh

Two slices sandwich-size meat

One medium pork chop

One-quarter pound hamburger patty

One-half chicken breast

One unbreaded three-ounce fish filet

Cooked meat the size of a deck of cards

(To reduce the fat content of poultry, remove the skin)

Fats, oils, and sweets group:

This group supplies few nutrients and mostly calories

Limit dressings on salads to one or two tablespoons, or use low-fat or fat-free

Limit spreads, toppings, gravies, and sauces

Limit cream cheese, sour cream, and margarine, or use low-fat or fat-free

Drink diet soft drinks to reduce sugar

Eat candies in moderation

Most of the selections should come from the bottom three groups of the pyramid, which are the vegetable group, the fruit group, and the bread, cereal, rice, and pasta group. Eat a variety of foods from each group since no food supplies all the nutrients needed by the body. Choose foods to meet the body's needs by controlling calories, fat, sodium, and cholesterol.

Eating right means ordering healthy food and smaller portions in a restaurant. If you find it hard to get what you need in the restaurants at truck stops, purchase a portable cooler to carry nonfat yogurt, fruit, and vegetables for breakfast, snacks, and from time to time, even lunch. The bonus there is that you can save a considerable amount of money by eating foods from a cooler rather than eating fast foods or at restaurants.

The following is an example of a healthy day's eating.

Breakfast:

Item	Calories
Yogurt, nonfat, one cup	225
Banana, one medium	105
Apple, one medium	80
Orange juice, one cup	85
Total calories	**495**

Lunch:

Item	Calories
Chicken, roasted, three ounces, without skin	95
Potato, baked, one medium	100
Sour cream, nonfat for potato	20
Corn, one cup, no butter	90
Salad, mixed greens with nonfat dressing	100
Biscuit, one, two inches across, no butter	105
Total Calories	**510**

Dinner:

Item	Calories
Fish, baked, three ounces	95
Potatoes, boiled, one cup, no butter	65
Vegetables, mixed, one cup, no butter	100
Roll, dinner, one, no butter	85
Salad, mixed greens, nonfat dressing	100
Total Calories	**445**

Snacks:

Item	Calories
Bagels, two	200
Apple, one medium	80
Banana, one medium	105
Peach, one medium	20
Celery and carrot sticks, eight	10
Strawberries, five berries	20
Total Calories	**435**

Total calories for the day: 1,885

To keep your weight down, combine lower calorie intake with regular exercise. Try to walk 30 minutes a day. Not only will that burn about 100 calories, it'll make you feel good and kind of kick-start your day.

The contents of this chapter were adapted from Shaw, A., Fulton, L., Davis, C., & Hogbin, M. Using the food guide pyramid: A resource for nutrition educators. Washington, DC: U.S. Department of Agriculture Center for Nutrition Policy and Promotion (CNPP). Available at http://www.usda.gov/cnpp/960201.pdf.

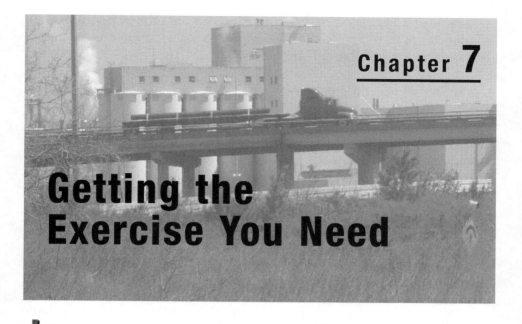

Chapter 7

Getting the Exercise You Need

Joe, who was raised on a ranch on the eastern plains of Colorado, was always active as a young man. He didn't need an exercise program; all he did was exercise. Help vaccinate the cattle. Help shear the sheep. Help build fences. Help load the hay. Help stack the hay in the barn. Help stack the cattle feed in the barn. Help feed the cattle. He didn't need an exercise program; exercise was his life.

In the summer when Joe wasn't working, he was playing. He would walk for miles in the big hay fields with his dog Buck, hunting rabbits. Sometimes, he would not take a gun and he would run with Buck across the fields, chasing rabbits. He loved to do this in the spring when the grass was beginning to grow, when the grass was first turning green after its long winter's nap, when the afternoon sun felt good on his back, not like the summer sun that would almost beat you down.

He and Buck would run for miles across the fields and along a little stream that ran beside the dirt road that led to town. And he loved to catch catfish from the little stream and then help his mom fry them to a golden brown for supper. He didn't need an exercise program. All Joe did was exercise.

In high school, he played football in the fall, basketball in the winter, and ran track in the spring. He attended the local community college where he studied range management, ran on the cross-country team in the fall, and ran on the track team in the spring. He didn't need an exercise program. All Joe did was exercise.

Then the drought came and cattle prices went down the drain.

Joe dropped out of college and got married. He and his wife had two kids. And he went to truck driving school. Joe was smart and he was a hard worker. He soon hooked up with an over-the-road carrier. No more running track. No more running with his dog, Buck. No more running along the little stream coursing beside the dirt road that led to town. No more running in the fields. Buck got old, went blind, and had to be put down.

For Joe, life became pretty much the same from day to day: drive and eat and sleep.

The years passed. And Joe, who ate the food his mom cooked and who loved every bite, still eats that same kind of food. Too many fried foods. Too much fat. Not enough fiber. Not enough vegetables. Not enough fruit. Not enough beans, cereals, rice, and pasta. Not enough water. Joe has gone from 145 pounds when he was in college to 210 pounds. Joe has gone from size 32 jeans to 38, and the 38s are getting a little tight around the middle.

Every time Joe takes his physical exam, his blood pressure is a little bit higher. Joe read an article in the company newsletter about diabetes that said if you were overweight, you could get diabetes. Joe knows that if you take insulin for your diabetes, you have to hang it up as a driver.

What Joe really needs is an exercise program.

Joe's situation is not unlike that of many truck drivers. A life filled with healthy exercise is replaced with a sedentary life when the transition is made to truck driving.

Lack of exercise is often compounded by other unhealthy habits such as smoking. Smoking substantially increases the risk of cardiovascular disease, is linked to about 30 percent of all cancer deaths, and is the leading cause of chronic lung disease.

If you have excessive body weight, you are also at risk for high blood pressure. In fact, almost every study of factors that influence blood pressure regulations has identified weight as the strongest predictor of high blood pressure.

High blood pressure, also known as hypertension, increases your risk of heart disease, renal failure, and stroke. It is a chronic disease in the U.S. affecting 50 million persons. It is estimated that in up to 50 percent of the adults in the U.S. whose hypertension is managed through pharmaceuticals, the need for drug therapy could be alleviated with only modest reduction in body weight.

Part 391 of the Code of Federal Regulations prescribes the maximum blood pressure level of commercial vehicle drivers as 160/90 mm Hg. As a result, we would expect a lower prevalence of hypertension because of these requirements; yet studies have shown that there is a higher prevalence of hypertension in truck drivers.

Aside from eating right, you can prevent excessive weight and high blood pressure by exercising regularly. Medical research has shown that physical activity can reduce the risk of many diseases including heart disease, high blood pressure, osteoporosis, diabetes, and breast and colon cancer, as well as reduce the risk of psychological illnesses such as depression, anxiety, and stress

You know what it takes to keep your truck running smoothly. The same principle is true for your body. You need an exercise program.

According to the Centers for Disease Control and Prevention (CDC), persons of all ages should have a minimum of 30 minutes of moderate exercise per day (such as brisk walking). This exercise can be broken into three 10-minutes periods and still provide a training effect.

A good exercise program could include three parts: walking, strength training, and flexibility.

Walking

Walk briskly (not a leisurely stroll, but not so hard that you can't carry on a conversation) for 30 minutes every day five days a week. If you are on a tight schedule, break it up into three 10-minute segments.

Other physical activities such as riding a stationary bike, swimming, mowing the grass, spading the garden, or skating—if they are done for at least 30 minutes—can substitute for a 30-minute walk.

Here's what some drivers say they do for walking exercise.

- I always walk facing the traffic and carry a flashlight with me at night.

- I ride a stationary bike for 30 minutes.

- I jump rope in the parking lot.

- When I inspect my rig after stopping to eat or rest, I walk around it ten times.

- At a truck stop, I always park as far away as I can, so I can get in some extra walking.

- In the winter, I like to chop firewood when I am at home.

- When I am at home, I like to walk and run with my kids. This gives me another workout and gives me some much needed time with my kids.

- I play basketball with my kids.

- I do some kind of sport with my family such as tennis, softball, golf, swimming, or hiking; anything to be together and to keep moving.

Strength Training

Many persons think that strength training is only for athletes or body-builders. However, research now shows that strength training can provide significant benefits to most adults. These include:

 Increasing muscle mass. As muscle mass increases, the body burns more calories, thereby helping lose fat.

 Preserving bone density. As adults get older, both males and females lose bone density, making the bones susceptible to fractures.

Protecting the major joints from injury. Many drivers suffer from back and shoulder pain. Making these joints stronger can reduce the pain.

 Improving balance.

 Reducing falls.

 Improving a person's ability to do work.

Strength training causes muscles to shorten against a resistance such as a dumbbell, your own weight, or ankle weights. This overloading of a muscle forces it to build more muscle mass and increase in strength. The key is to progressively increase the resistance to allow the muscles to adapt and develop more strength and endurance.

The intensity of a workout (how hard you are working) is determined by the resistance and how many times you repeat the activity. One repetition is doing a movement one time. When first starting any kind of exercise program, the intensity should be low. The first three weeks, do five repetitions of each activity. After the first three weeks, the number of repetitions should be increased by two per week until 20 repetitions are reached. It is not necessary to do more than 20 repetitions. Repeat the workout two times per week. Skip two or three days between workouts.

You only need two dumbbells and ankle weights to do strength training. Purchase dumbbells that allow you to change the weight by adding more individual plates to each side. Suggested starting weight is five to 15 pounds.

Your training program should include:

Squats. While holding onto something sturdy, bend your knees until your thighs are parallel to the ground. Do five repetitions per workout for the first three weeks. Then increase by two per two-week period until you reach 20 repetitions. After a period of time if the squats are too easy, hold weights in the hands to increase the difficulty.

Push-Ups. Lie on your stomach, feet together, and hands by your shoulders. While holding your back rigid, push with your arms until they are straight. If it has been a while since you have done push-ups, you might try modified push-ups for the first few weeks. In a modified push-up, you push with your weight on your knees rather than on your toes. Do five repetitions per workout for the first three weeks, and then increase by two per two-week period until you reach 20 repetitions.

Back Extensions. While lying on your stomach with hands under your chin, keep your feet on the floor while you slowly lift your chest about five inches off the floor. Hold for five seconds and then slowly return to the starting position. Do five repetitions per workout for the first three weeks, and then increase by two per two-week period until you reach 20 repetitions.

Crunches. While lying on your back with your knees bent, feet flat on the floor and arms crossed on the chest, slowly lift your head, shoulders, and upper back off the floor. Hold for two seconds and slowly return to the starting position. Do five repetitions per workout for the first three weeks, and then increase by two per two-week period until you reach 20 repetitions.

Standing Leg Curl. While standing upright and holding onto something sturdy with ankle weights on each ankle, slowly raise your right heel toward your buttocks. Hold for five seconds and then lower it to the starting position. Repeat the movement with your left ankle. This is one repetition. Do five repetitions per workout for the first three weeks, and then increase by two per two-week period until you reach 20 repetitions.

Bicep Curl. Sitting or standing, hold a weight in each hand with your arms straight down at your sides. Bending at the elbows, slowly raise the weights to your shoulders. Hold for five seconds and slowly return to the starting position. This is one repetition. Do five repetitions per workout for the first three weeks, and then increase by two per two-week period until you reach 20 repetitions.

Triceps Curl. Standing or sitting with a weight in each hand and the arms extended above the head, slowly bend the arms at the elbow, lowering the weights until the forearms are parallel to the floor. Hold for five seconds and slowly raise the weights to the starting position. This is one repetition. Do five repetitions per workout for the first three weeks, and then increase by two per two-week period until you reach 20 repetitions.

Shoulder Press. Standing or sitting with a weight in each hand and the arms at the shoulders, slowly extend the arms above the head. Hold for five seconds and then slowly return the weights to the shoulders. This is one repetition. Do five repetitions per workout for the first three weeks, and then increase by two per two-week period until you reach 20 repetitions.

Upright Row. Standing, holding a weight in each hand at the front of the thighs, slowly raise both weights to armpit level, keeping the elbows higher than your hands. Hold for five seconds and slowly lower the weight to the starting position. This is one repetition. Do five repetitions per workout for the first three weeks, and then increase by two per two-week period until you reach 20 repetitions.

Here's what some drivers said about strength training:

- After I got my shoulders and back stronger, I had no pain after driving long hours.

- I do my crunches and push-ups in my cab before I go to sleep. It helps me sleep better.

- I tighten my stomach and butt muscles while driving, hold for 30 seconds, and then release.

- Sometimes, I take my weights with me into the lounge at truck stops so I can watch TV while I lift.

- I try to do one of my weekly weight workouts at home because I am so busy on the road.

One of the truck stops I go to regularly has a gym so I work out there. Sure is nice.

 When I am at home, my whole family lifts weights with me.

 When I climb on my rig to wash it, I can tell my arms and legs are stronger.

 When I mowed my grass for the first time this spring, I could tell I was a lot stronger.

 My wife told me I looked younger!

Flexibility

Flexibility has been defined as the range of motion available in a joint or group of joints. It is the ability to move, bend, twist, and stretch easily.

The following are some benefits of being flexible.

 Body moves with less effort.

Less lower-back, shoulder, and arm pain.

Fewer injuries to knees, hips, back, and shoulder areas.

Reduces muscle tension and makes the body more relaxed.

Promotes blood circulation.

Prevents loss of flexibility that happens with age.

A flexibility program could include the following.

Warming up. Always do flexibility activities after you are warmed up, at the end of walking, or after strength training.

Chest. Reach behind your back and clasp your hands together. Lift arms as high as possible and hold for five seconds. Repeat five times

Arm and Shoulder. Standing facing a wall or side of your truck with right palm on the wall or truck, hand rotated so fingers point down and thumb pointed towards outside of body, rotate the body as far to the left as you can. Hold for five seconds. Repeat five times. Switch arms and repeat the activity.

How often. Every time you work out, do the flexibility activities.

Here's what some drivers said about flexibility:

 I feel more relaxed after doing flexibility activities.

I don't have as much back and shoulder pain.

The last time I was home, I was working on my car and I could reach places I could never reach before.

I can scratch my back better.

Finally, let's look at some general things drivers said about exercise:

 Health is 100% related to safety. And physical activity is essential to health. We need to be getting more exercise and get moving more on a daily basis.

Trucks are getting easier to drive. We don't have to load and unload, and we are getting less exercise on the job, so we need to get more exercise.

Anything I do to move is exercise. Twenty extra steps is better than none.

When I am on the road, I do a lot of stretching exercises. It keeps my back from hurting.

It's a habit now. I park farthest away wherever I go.

I do my arm exercises before I go to bed. It helps me sleep better.

Walking makes me feel good. I really like to walk in the woods, or along a river or lake.

Chapter 8

Medical Care and Wellness on the Road

Danny, almost 40, has been driving for close to 20 years, and likes his job.

What he doesn't like is being on the road and feeling too sick to drive. "I was 1,000 miles from home and came down with a case of kidney stones," he said. "Not much fun to be sick by yourself." Luckily, Danny's bout with kidney stones is the most critical health care problem he's had in 20 years. "Looks like my luck finally ran out," he said.

Health care is important at any time in your life, but when you spend most of your days traveling America's highways, whenever you do have a health problem, getting help may not always be easy.

On the other hand, staying healthy isn't difficult for professional drivers because the Department of Transportation (DOT) requires a complete physical every two years. In many cases, these biennial checkups will catch the early stages of a health condition before it grows into a big problem.

The Federal Motor Carriers Safety Regulations direct any driver who becomes ill and not capable of handling the truck to pull over and seek medical care immediately. That rules out trying to drive when you're ill.

In most cases, if you become ill while you're on the road, and if you work for a carrier that provides health insurance coverage, a call to the human relations (HR) office should give you information about which doctors, clinics, and hospitals—wherever you are—are covered by your plan, will accept your insurance, or are approved by your insurance provider.

If you carry your own policy, you may want to use an Internet search to find out what health care providers in the area will accept your coverage. One quick way is to enter the keyword "hospital directory" on AOL and then shop for medical care by state, city, and finally zip code.

Another way to find health care help on the Web is to go to the California Medical Transport site for locating hospitals, medical groups, and clinics by state, city, or town.

MedicinePlanet, an m-Health site, is not only a new buzz word but also a growing number of Web sites offering health care service and information, and health care by means of mobile devices. Offering sites to everyone, MedicinePlanet provides health information to travelers, immunization recommendations, preventative health care tips, local health care providers, and suggested products and insurance, all for under $5 per month.

The Travelers Emergency Network (TEN) is a group offering 24-hour access to medical experts, emergency evacuation, and other services. Membership in TEN provides access to medical facilities around the world as well as referrals, medical monitoring, and emergency case coordination. It is not insurance and costs $129 per year.

Veterans can always go to the nearest Veterans Administration hospital for care. If you need directions to the nearest center, consult the VA Web site at http://www.va.gov/. Here you will find VA facilities listed by state. VA facilities are located in all of the 50 states, Washington, DC, and off-shore in Guam, the Philippines, Puerto Rico, and the Virgin Islands.

HEALTH CARE CLINICS IN TRUCK STOPS: A NEW TREND

Artel Medical Centers was begun in 1997 with the idea of building medical clinics in existing truck stops, according to Artel president Steve Kellam.

"The model we initially used has changed and now we license the Artel Medical model to clinics that are situated in truck stops and in locations designed to serve a broader population, including truckers," Kellam said.

The concept was begun by Kellam, a veteran of the transportation industry, who saw a real need for accessible health care for drivers as they crisscrossed the country. "A lot of folks in medicine today aren't aware of the requirements placed on truck drivers and the care necessary for them to maintain their health," Kellam said. "That was why we started, but we changed our approach because we found we could reach more truckers if we licensed our product to others rather than building clinics across the country."

In Rochelle, Illinois, for example, the Petro Travel Plaza has an on-site clinic, which offers ample parking and is open to truckers and travelers. "The hospital in Rochelle actually owns the clinic and we support them with our management and with our model," Kellam said.

One important factor often missing in an over-the-road driver's health care is consistency and availability of a driver's medical records. Kellam said he has tried to address this issue through Artel's Hapinet System. "When truck drivers go to a one of our licensed clinics, their medical record information can be obtained through password and security technology," Kellam explained. "In other words, their information is portable."

Today, many drivers carry their medical information with them, showing drug tests and results as well as the results of their most recent DOT physical. "Sometimes this paperwork gets lost," Kellam continued. "If they have been seen by any of our clinics, they can go and request copies for their on-board information packet and we'll give them printouts."

Some of the Artel clinics—located across the country from Portland, Oregon to Baltimore, Maryland—have been licensed to accept insurance. However, if they don't, they provide drivers with a form so they can be reimbursed for their out-of-pocket medical expenses while they're on the road.

Another service Artel provides trucking companies is their "Passing Zone" product, offered through more than 2,000 clinics across the country. "This is how we help companies manage their compliance,"

Kellam said. "We set up this network so that when truckers need to take drug tests, we guarantee they can get to a clinic to take the test, wherever they are in the country."

The same service provides physicians, physician's assistants, or nurse practitioners licensed to conduct DOT exams at the carrier's facility to provide physicals for new drivers. "This makes it more efficient for the carrier and the driver," Kellam said.

Other services provided by Artel include DOT/CDL physicals and compliance testing, medical and nonmedical services including illness care, minor health routine preventative care, and health promotions. Artel also provides consolidated billing service, high-security computerized medical records, and health care promotions such as flu shots, blood pressure testing, and other tests.

For more information, visit Artel's Web site at http://www.artelmedical.com.

HEALTH CARE THROUGH THE WORLD WIDE WEB

Years ago, when someone in the family became ill, there was usually someone in the neighborhood who was medically minded and who could make recommendations to help the patient recover. Later, families referred to medical encyclopedias or, for children's illnesses, they read Dr. Spock's book.

Today, more people are going online to get medical information from the Internet. Many Web sites now offer information from libraries at major medical centers. Those interested in learning more about an illness or chronic disease can also find information on the latest research in these areas and connect with others who have similar medical conditions through chat rooms, all from the convenience and comfort of their homes, schools or the public library.

But as more and more people consult the Web for medical information, the question arises, "How do you know if information is reliable and accurate?"

Medical professionals will tell you the best medical Web sites to browse are those associated with professional societies or major medical schools. For example, if you need information on asthma, the American Academy of Allergy, Asthma and Immunology is a good, reliable resource. And the National Institutes of Health's (NIH) government Web site offers links to hundreds of equally reliable medical information sites.

Med Help International, a nonprofit organization, is dedicated to helping patients find the highest quality medical information in the world today. The group, which can be found at http://medhlp.netusa.net/home.htm, offers patients the necessary tools to make informed treatment decisions within short time lines dictated by their illness or disease.

Virtual Medical Center for Patients is a collection of information and professional medical support gathered from the best medical organizations and experts in the world. The group also hosts medical forums for topics that include addiction, breast cancer, child behavioral health, dermatology, family practice, gastroenterology, heart, hepatitis, liver diseases, mental health, neurology, neurosurgery, and respiratory disorders.

Med Help International also provides a comprehensive consumer health information library, and question-and-answer forums where patients can ask questions of leading physicians and health care professionals. A patient-to-patient network is also available as well as daily medical and health news.

The Mayo Clinic, long a respected center for health and medical care, has a Web site called Mayo Clinic Health O@sis. This site is directed by a team of Mayo physicians, scientists, writers, and educators, and features specific centers for various medical problems. These include allergy and asthma, Alzheimer's, cancer, and heart centers.

If you're not sure about the site, ask questions like, "How often has this site been updated?" "Does it link to other Web sites?" "Is it affiliated with major medical institutions?"

One recommended site is "Healthfinder", a Web site that offers much information on many subjects. Healthfinder can be located at http://www.healthfinder.gov. But when in doubt about your health, the first step should be to consult your physician. Then use online information to help you understand the problem. Using the Internet is never a good substitute for being seen by a physician or other medical personnel.

DON'T FORGET DENTAL CARE

To be in good health, you must have good dental and oral hygiene. Being on the road full time is no excuse not to see your dentist at least once a year; better yet, once every six months.

If you are a smoker or use smokeless tobacco, the dentist will also conduct an examination to make certain there is no evidence of oral cancer.

It is important to realize that infected teeth can sometimes cause other problems in the body. Good dental hygiene can help head off these unexpected problems.

Nothing could be worse than a toothache, mid-trip. These dental emergencies—and the possible loss of a tooth or multiple teeth—may be avoided with consistent daily care and periodic trips to the dentist for exams and cleaning.

And as a public relations point, nothing is worse than the breath of someone with decayed or decaying teeth. Keep your breath fresh when dealing with customers and take care of your teeth at all times. They're the only ones you'll ever have, and dentures can cost a week's salary or more.

YOUR ANNUAL DOT PHYSICAL: A GOOD TOOL FOR STAYING HEALTHY

Regulation 391.43 of the Federal Motor Carrier Safety Administration's regulations outlines the medical examination for professional drivers that must be done every two years.

The purpose of the history taken by the examiner and the physical examination conducted by the examiner is to detect the presence of any new physical and mental defects. A history of certain defects may be cause for rejection, or may indicate the need for certain lab tests or a closer examination.

Physical defects may be recorded that do not, because of their character or degree, indicate that certification of physical fitness should be denied. However, these defects should be discussed with the driver so he or she can be advised to take the necessary steps to ensure correction, particularly when neglect could lead to a condition that could affect his/her ability to drive safely.

The following parts should be completed by the medical examiner performing the physical:

Appearance. The examiner is directed to note any overweight, any posture defect, perceptible limp, tremor, or other defects that could be caused by alcoholism, thyroid irregularities, or other illness. The FMCSR requires that no driver use a narcotic or other habit-forming drugs.

Eyes. If the applicant wears corrective lenses, these should be used during the visual testing. If the driver habitually wears contact lenses while driving, there should be sufficient evidence to indicate that he/she has good tolerance and is well adapted to the use of contact lenses. The use of contacts should be noted on the record. Drivers who have lost one eye are not qualified to operate commercial vehicles under existing FMCSRs.

Ears. Note any evidence of middle ear disease, symptoms of dizziness, or Meniere's Syndrome. When recording hearing, record distance from patient at which a force whispered voice can first be heard. If audiometer is used to test hearing, record decibel loss at 500 Hz., 1,000 Hz., and 2,000 Hz.

Throat. Note any evidence of disease, deformities of the throat likely to interfere with eating or breathing, or any condition of the larynx that could interfere with the safe operation of a CMV.

Chest and Heart. Stethoscopic examination is required. Note murmurs and arrhythmias, and any past or present history of cardiovascular disease of a variety known to be accompanied by syncope, dypsnea, collapse, enlarged heart, or congestive heart failure. EKG is required when stethoscopic findings so indicate.

Blood Pressure. Record using a blood pressure cuff. If the blood pressure is consistently above 160/90 mm.Hg., further tests may be necessary to determine whether driver is qualified to operate CMV.

Lungs. If lung disease is detected, state whether active or arrested. If arrested, a physician must give an opinion as to how long it has been arrested.

Gastrointestinal System. Note any diseases of the esophagus, stomach, small, or large intestine.

Abdomen. Note any wounds, scars, injuries, or weakness of muscles of abdominal walls sufficient to interfere with normal function. Any hernia should be noted, including how long it has been present and if adequately contained by truss.

Abnormal Masses. If present, note location and if tender, whether or not applicant knows how long they have been present. If diagnosis suggests the condition may interfere with control and safe operation of CMV, more tests should be made before applicant can be certified.

Tenderness. When tenderness is noted, state where it is most pronounced and the suspected cause. If diagnosis suggests condition may interfere with control and safe operation of CMV, more tests should be made.

Genitourinary. A urinalysis is required. Acute infections of the genitourinary tract should be noted as well as indications from urinalysis of uncontrolled diabetes, symptomatic albumin urea in the urine, or other findings indicating health conditions that may interfere with control and safe operation of CMV will disqualify applicant from operating a CMV.

Neurological. Pupillary reflexes should be reported for both light and accommodation. Knee jerks are to be reported absent only when not obtainable on reinforcement and as increased when foot is actually lifted from the floor, following a light blow to the patella. Sensory vibratory and positional abnormalities should be noted.

Extremities. Care should be taken to examine upper and lower extremities. Record the loss or impairment of a leg, foot, toe, arm, hand, or fingers. Note any and all deformities, the presence of atrophy, semiparalysis or paralysis, or varicose veins. If a hand or finger deformity exists, determine whether sufficient grasp is present to enable driver to secure and maintain a grip on the steering wheel. If a leg deformity exists, determine whether there is sufficient mobility and strength present to enable the driver to operate pedals properly. Particular attention should be given to, and a record should be made of, any impairment or structural defect which may interfere with the driver's ability to operate a CMV safely.

Spine. Note deformities, limitation of motion or history of pain, injuries, or disease in cervical or lumbar spine region. If findings dictate, X-ray or other examination should be used to diagnose congenital or acquired defects.

Rectogenital Studies: Diseases or conditions causing discomfort should be evaluated carefully to determine the extent to which the condition might be handicapping while lifting, pulling, or during periods of prolonged driving that might be necessary as part of the driver's duties.

Laboratory and Other Special Findings: Urinalysis is required, as well as other tests, as medical history and physical findings may indicate as necessary. A serological test is required if applicant has a history of venereal disease or findings indicating the possibility of latent syphilis. Other studies deemed necessary by the examiner may also be ordered.

Diabetes. If insulin is necessary to control a diabetic condition, the driver is not qualified to operate a CMV. If mild diabetes is noted and is stabilized by use of a hypoglycemic drug and a diet that can be obtained while the driver is on duty, it should not be disqualifying. However, the driver must remain under adequate medical supervision.

The examiner will ask the driver if there is any history of head or spinal injuries; seizures, convulsions, or fainting; extensive confinement by illness or injury; heart disease; tuberculosis; syphilis; gonorrhea; diabetes; stomach ulcer; nervous stomach; rheumatic fever; asthma; kidney disease; muscular disease; any other diseases or permanent defect from illness or injury; and psychiatric disorder and any other nervous disorder.

Once the examination and the medical history is complete, the examiner will sign a certificate, stating that the driver has met all requirements and is certified to safely control and operate a CMV.

Chapter 9

Trucker Skills

DRIVER FATIGUE

A sleepy driver is a dangerous driver. Every year, thousands of accidents are caused by drivers who were too tired to drive. Fatigue is like drugs or alcohol: it impairs your judgment and increases your reaction time. In its most common form, it dulls your senses enough to affect your judgment as you approach other vehicles or make a turn. You may approach too fast or not brake in time, causing a collision. In more extreme cases of fatigue, you could literally fall asleep at the wheel and leave the road, rolling the truck over or striking another vehicle or object at high speed.

The most dangerous part of fatigue is not recognizing it. Many drivers will claim they are fit to drive when really they're not. That's why your best weapon against fatigue is knowledge. First, you need to understand what causes fatigue. Second, understand your own body and when you need rest.

Fatigue is caused by lack of sleep, or long periods of repetitive activity and/or strenuous physical exercise. When the hours of service rules were first written in the 1930s, truck driving was more strenuous physically than it is today. Rest was required mostly to give the driver's body a break. Modern drivers can still get tired from long hours at the wheel, or loading and unloading the truck, but fatigue today is mostly caused by insufficient or inadequate sleep.

All humans crave sleep. It's one of our three basic needs besides food and water. Scientific research has showed that starving for sleep over a long period is fatal.

Scientists aren't quite sure why, but they know sleep plays an essential restorative role for our brains. We need a certain amount of sleep every day to stay healthy.

Your body rests while you sleep, but your brain doesn't. It actually is extremely busy, cycling between a number of different sleep stages. There are two main sleep stages: nonrapid eye movement (NREM) and rapid eye movement (REM). There are four stages of NREM sleep, each deeper than the previous level. After a period of NREM sleep (usually about two hours), we go into REM sleep, the time when we do most of our dreaming.

If you are driving while tired, you may experience a "microsleep" where you nod off for a few seconds. In these brief periods of unconsciousness, you have fallen into the first light stage of NREM sleep. If you continue to drive and become much more fatigued, you will lapse into even deeper NREM sleep and it will be more difficult to rouse yourself out of it. Microsleeps are dangerous. A lot can happen in two or three seconds at 60 mph. If microsleep occurs, it's a good warning for you to get off the road and get some rest.

Most scientists agree that everyone needs between seven and nine hours sleep in every 24-hour period. But for the sleep to be effective, you need to spend some time in deep NREM and REM stages. That's why continuity of sleep is more important than how much total time you are asleep.

Assuming you don't have a sleep disorder (we'll talk more about that later), three factors will determine your level of tiredness at any one time.

1. **Age.** Older people tend to need more sleep.

2. **The amount of prior sleep.** Without enough sleep over a series of days, a sleep debt accrues. It can take a long time to erase that debt, particularly if you continue to short-change yourself.

3. **Circadian rhythms.** Everyone has an internal clock which slows and speeds the body's metabolism at certain times of the day. Early afternoons and early mornings are the body's natural "low" times. These rhythms are upset when you change your work shifts and sleep patterns. That's why people suffer jet lag when they travel through different time zones.

There are a lot of myths about fatigue prevention. Chemical substances such as caffeine can act as stimulants and keep you awake, but they are only temporary. When they wear off, you'll be even more tired than before.

Sleep is the ultimate cure. To get the right amount of continuous sleep regularly, you should try to find a good sleep environment. Ideally, it should be dark since darkness is one of the body's natural cues to sleep. Temperature is also important. If it's too cold or too hot, it's difficult to stay asleep. Most people prefer an environment between 65°F and 75°F. Finally, try to find a quiet place. Noises, particularly those that are irregular like traffic noise, can prevent good, deep sleep.

Getting the rest you need can often be difficult, given the irregular schedules you often deal with. Here are some things you can do to stay as alert and as safe as possible.

 When you are traveling an interstate route, keep a watch or clock on your home time zone so that you are able to keep your body clock on the same schedule as much as possible.

Take rest breaks at least once every four or five hours. Even if you don't feel tired, it will give you time to relax and refocus.

Try to avoid driving early in the afternoon (1 a.m. to 2 p.m.) or early in the morning (1 a.m. to 4 a.m.) when your body goes through a natural drowsy period. If you must drive, be especially careful.

 Stay fit by exercising regularly. It will allow you to sleep more soundly and keep you more alert.

 Try to get at least seven hours of good sleep in every 24-hour period.

Take brief naps (less than 40 minutes) when you feel tired. If you go longer, you will get into deeper REM sleep, which is harder to get out of and will leave you drowsy for some time after you wake up.

Be careful about using caffeine. Instead of drinking it constantly, save it for when you need it most.

SLEEP DISORDERS

The evidence is clear: Sleep is the only real remedy for fatigue. But for many truck drivers, something as simple as sleep can be difficult to obtain. That's because many drivers have sleep disorders. Even if they can make time to sleep, it may not be good sleep and can leave them more tired than before.

Many people have trouble sleeping. Surveys conducted in the 1970s suggest about 50 million adults in the U.S. have difficulty getting the rest they need. Various disorders can cause bad sleep including insomnia (often related to stress), narcolepsy (excessive sleepiness related to brain malfunctions), and leg twitches (legs jerk repeatedly during sleep that keep sufferers awake).

But sleep apnea is probably the most common disorder. It affects at least 18 million American adults, or one to four percent of the total population. Surveys have shown it could be as high as 35% of truck drivers, or seven times higher than the national average.

Apnea sufferers are definitely bigger accident risks. A 1988 study showed the accident rate among them was eight times higher than those without apnea. Apnea is also a health risk because it increases the potential for heart problems, stroke, and memory loss.

Apnea is actually a breathing problem. From the Latin word meaning "no breath," sleep apnea is any condition in which the flow of air to the lungs stops for 10 seconds or longer.

There are three types of apnea: obstructive apnea (OSA), central apnea, and mixed apnea. OSA is by far the most common. It occurs when a part of the airway collapses during sleep, preventing the sufferer from breathing. Much of the problem can be traced back to the design of the pharynx, the passage from the tip of the nose to the voice box. We use it to swallow, talk, and breathe. For each of these functions, the pharynx needs to take a different form. It needs to be stiff so you can breathe, but collapsible so you can swallow and talk.

When you fall asleep, your muscles aren't as active. The pharynx narrows and makes it harder to breathe. If it narrows enough, you start to snore. In apnea cases, it closes altogether. Since our brain is programmed for survival, it will sense the lack of oxygen and wake the person briefly (three to 10 seconds) every minute or so to take a breath or two. Unfortunately, sufferers aren't aware of these constant arousals. They wake up in the morning and think they have slept the whole night, when really they have had very little effective sleep.

Truck drivers are predisposed to be OSA sufferers because they have certain physical characteristics. These include being middle-aged and male; overweight; a thick neck (over size 17); a small jaw; large tonsils; and a deviated septum (the dividing wall in the nose is crooked).

Here are some warning signs that indicate you may have OSA:

 Loud, heavy snoring that is interrupted by periods of silence or pauses in breathing.

 Gasping or choking during sleep.

 Restless sleep.

● Excessive sleepiness or fatigue during the day.

● Anxiety or depression.

● Frequent morning headaches.

● Memory loss.

● Irritability.

If you think you have OSA or another sleep disorder, see a doctor or sleep specialist. There are hundreds of sleep clinics around the country. The American Academy of Sleep Medicine (507/287-6006) can help find one.

At the clinic, you will generally go through a number of painless tests to determine if you have a disorder and what type it is. If you are diagnosed with apnea, there are a number of treatments. The easiest are losing weight, exercising regularly, sleeping in a different position, and using nasal sprays to clear the nose. If none of these solves the problem, you may need to use a device called continuous positive airway pressure (CPAP) while you sleep. This consists of a small blower connected by hose to a mask over your nose. While you sleep, the blower sends a constant stream of air through the nose and into the throat to keep the airway open. The amount of air pressure needed is determined by a doctor, often during a sleep study. It can be readjusted if you lose or gain weight. The CPAP units are quite small and can easily be carried with you. Surgery to clear the passageway is used only as a last resort because of the risks and possible complications.

MOM AND POP TRUCK STOPS SERVE UP A LITTLE BIT OF HOME WITH FUEL AND FOOD

More than 20 years ago, the Dorsett family opened Dorsett's 221 Truckstop at exit 221 on Interstate 35 in Buda (pronounced Bew-da), TX. With a full-service restaurant as its centerpiece, the 14-acre mom and pop included fleet service, parking, a fuel center, and a two-story motel.

After the restaurant burned in 1999, the family sold the motel and garage so they could focus on their newly-restored restaurant and expanded driver services.

"We've always been known for our homestyle food and our friendly service," said Sandy Dorsett, restaurant manager. "And our customers know we make chili, beef stew, and chicken and dumplings fresh, twice a day. We've used the same recipe and have been doing things the same way for 20 years."

The restaurant is also a favorite stop for truckers who look forward to pancakes the size of saddle blankets, and biscuits and gravy guaranteed to melt in your mouth.

Two spacious dining rooms are divided by a fish tank that's home to fish caught by the Dorsett children, and computer plug-ins are available for drivers who want to eat and take care of business at the same time.

"We're thinking about adding a station for computers adjacent to the drivers room," Dorsett said, "and we also have a TV lounge with video games and a load board, faxes and copiers, Com-Check, showers, laundry room, scales, and parking. Fleet service and the motel are less than a block away."

But Dorsett's is known for something more than food and fuel. "With Buda being a small town, we're the down-home, little-town restaurant for our neighbors as well as a home for the drivers when they're on the road," Dorsett said, "and they tell us, it feels like home the minute they walk in the door."

These "family ties" often go deeper than Dorsett's platter-sized chicken fried steak smothered in gravy and tall glasses of freshly brewed iced tea. "One evening we got a call from a dispatcher, telling us one of his drivers had scheduled a stop here," she recalled. "The driver's family—a pregnant wife and little girl—had been killed in a tragic accident a few hours earlier and the dispatcher wanted us to help him get home."

After gently breaking the news, the Dorsett family took the driver's keys, drove him to the airport, and bought his plane ticket home. "We do whatever we can when these drivers need help," Dorsett said, "and a lot of times, when homeless people or runaway kids get rides and then get dumped here, we're glad to help, however we can, whether it's just a cup of coffee and a burger or talking to a kid who walks in, looking lost, at 2 a.m., then buying them a bus ticket to go back home."

A few years ago, a pregnant team driver started early labor and stopped at Dorsett's. "The couple was traveling with their three kids, and when the paramedics were loading the lady onto a gurney for the hospital in San Marcos, she was worried about her kids. 'Don't worry, ma'am,' the paramedic said. 'Sandy and Ronnie Dorsett will take good care of them.' And we did—for three days—until mom and dad, the new baby, and their family could head home," Dorsett recalled.

"There are good people driving up and down our highways, and we get a lot of them here, from Mexico to Canada. And there's something new every day, which is probably why we love this business like we do."

Not willing to compete with the newer travel center chains, the Dorsett family is in the truck stop business to make a living. "We have a good reputation and we pride ourselves in being family-owned and operated," Dorsett said. "We don't allow table-to-table soliciting, we ask people to put on more clothes if they don't have enough on, and we keep our parking lot cleaned up. We like truckers and we like serving the hundreds of regulars who sit down at our tables each day. They're special people, simply the greatest you'd ever want to meet."

Chapter 10

Road Rage: A Deadly Game

ROAD RAGE:
THE ILLNESS OF THE NEW MILLENNIUM

Bob slows and eases his rig into line for the Border Patrol inspection. He glances at his watch. "If this doesn't take too long, I should be in San Antonio by midnight."

After the inspection, the miles glide by and as traffic increases, Bob knows he is nearing San Antonio. He slows for the Loop 1604 exit.

Bob knows this route well. He's driven it for the past 10 years.

East on Loop 1604 and then north, crossing over I-10, Bob can see the lights of the I-35 exit only a few miles ahead. "I wonder why I'm having that burning in my stomach again? "Well, here it is, I-35." Since NAFTA was signed in 1993, this 250 miles to Dallas right through the heart of Texas is one of the most traveled highways in the country, and it seems to Bob that most of it is under construction.

Bob eases up onto I-35. Shifting though the gears, he quickly gets up to cruising speed.

After a few miles, traffic gets worse. "Must be getting near New Braunfels." Wall to wall trucks, pickups, and SUVs. "These Texas guys love their pickups and SUVs." Construction on the left. Construction on the right. "I wonder why my arms and shoulders feel so tight?"

Narrow lanes. Concrete barriers on the left. Concrete barriers on the right. Headlights coming up fast. "Can't change lanes right now, buddy. Slow that rocket down! Now what's that fool doing, blinking his lights and honking his horn?"

Narrow lanes. Concrete barriers on the left. Concrete barriers on the right. Traffic on the left. Traffic on the right. Can't change lanes. "Sorry, buddy. Can't help you now." (Stomach burning, arms and shoulders hurting.)

"A gap ahead in the right lane. I think I can get this rig in it so that fool behind me can go on and not kill us all.

"Where is he? I don't see him. That fool's in my no-zone!"

About that time, the construction ended and a black dual-wheeled crewcab pickup roared past Bob on the inside shoulder, cut back in front of him, and slammed on his brakes.

Hitting his air brakes, Bob fought to keep his rig in his lane.

As Bob's rig slid toward a crash, the pickup lurched forward with the driver holding his hand out the window, nominating Bob for "number one," and disappeared into the night.

Fortunately, because of Bob's professional driving skills and the skills of other drivers around him, every one stayed upright and on the highway that night.

An isolated incident?   Unfortunately, no.

Aggressive Driving Leads to Road Rage

How big a problem is aggressive driving in the United States? Here is some data from the National Highway Traffic Safety Administration (NHTSA) regarding the problem of aggressive driving.

NHTSA defines aggressive driving as, "The operation of a motor vehicle in a manner that endangers or is likely to endanger persons or property." A traffic offense and not a criminal offense like "road rage."

Of the approximately 6,800,000 motor vehicle crashes that occur in the United States each year, a substantial number are estimated to be caused by aggressive driving.

1997 statistics compiled by NHTSA and the American Automobile Association show that almost 13,000 persons have been injured or killed since 1990 in crashes caused by aggressive driving.

In a recent survey sponsored by the NHTSA, over 60% of U.S. drivers said they consider unsafe driving practices a major threat to their personal safety.

About 30 percent of respondents said they felt their safety was threatened in the last month, while 67 percent felt this threat sometime during the last year.

Aggressive drivers are more likely to drink and drive.

More than half of those surveyed admitted to driving aggressively on occasions.

Ricardo Martinez, federal administrator of NHTSA, has declared that road rage is now the number-one traffic problem in the U.S.

What are other agencies and institutions reporting about this problem?

The New York Times reported a poll taken in Washington, DC showed that 42% of the residents rate aggressive drivers as the biggest threat on the road, even greater than drunk drivers.?

The American Automobile Association's Foundation for Traffic Safety released data in 1996 showing the average number of violent incidents reported between drivers in the U.S. has increased annually over the past eight years, 51% since 1990. In 1996, about 2,000 violent incidents were formally reported by police nationwide.

Many safety officials consider this the tip of a very large iceberg. They believe that for every aggressive driving incident serious enough to result in a police report or newspaper article, there are hundreds or thousands more that are never reported.

On an Internet site used by professional truck drivers, it was noted that most professional drivers regularly experience road rage incidents. Another popular Internet site revealed that 78% of drivers reported being verbally abused by four-wheelers. Another 21% reported that other drivers had tried to force them off the road.

So what is causing all this aggressive driving?

Generally, most safety experts agree that aggressive driving and road rage are a result of more cars, which leads to more traffic, which leads to more frustration, which leads to more stress, which leads to more anger, which leads to more hostility, which leads to more violence.

Jerry Smith, police chief of a town north of San Antonio that straddles I-35, summed up causes for increasing road rage like this:

"Stress, stress, and more stress. Stress about their jobs. Stress about their kids. Stress about their home life. Stress about the economy. Stress getting to and from their jobs. Sometimes, because of an accident on I-35, the traffic stops for an hour or more. When some people have that much stress, day after day, something has to give."

While many safety experts agree that more traffic causes more frustration, some experts think the road rage problem may come from other sources.

Dr. Leon James, professor of psychology at the University of Hawaii, in testimony given before the U.S. House Subcommittee, stated in part that,

> *"The car is not only an object of convenience, beauty, and status. It is also a cultural and psychological object, associated with the driver's internal mental and emotional dynamics, our ego.*
>
> *"Cars are an extension of the self, they are ego-laden objects that can be used both positively and negatively to get our own way on the road. The automobile offers us a means to exercise direct control over our environment. When we enter the car, we use it as an outlet for regaining control over our environment."*

So what does this mean to Bob, the professional driver, who is trying to make a living by driving on traffic-laden I-35 through the heart of Texas? To see how this affects Bob let's consider Ann.

> Ann lives in the hills about 30 miles north of San Antonio in an upscale neighborhood. She is married to James and they have two lovely children. Her kids are smart, go to a great school, and make good grades.

Sounds pretty good, huh? Well, everything is not all good for Ann. James, a salesman for a printing company, is gone from home Tuesday through Friday making sales calls. That means Ann has the primary responsibility for the children, the house, meal preparation, picking up the children after school, and soccer practice.

Well, that doesn't sound too bad. Ann and James do most of the grocery shopping on the weekends. They clean the house, look after the yard, do the laundry, and prepare many of the meals for the week, which are stored in the freezer until needed. Additionally, James golfs, Ann plays tennis, and they go to the kids' soccer games on weekends. Following church on Sunday morning, James reviews his assignments for the upcoming week, Ann prepares a presentation for work, the children study, and the weekend is gone.

A tight schedule? Yes, but not impossible. Oh, did I tell you that because of the heavy traffic, Ann has an hour commute in the mornings and evenings? I think I also forgot to tell you the road Ann takes to work is I-35, which is under construction all the way, and has been and will be under construction for years to come.

How bad is the traffic for Ann? "If I leave work at 5:00, I get home at 7:00. If I leave work at 6:00, I get home at 7:00. So I stay in the office and work until 6:00."

Is a picture of Ann beginning to develop here?

Highly organized, on a tight schedule, a hard worker trying to make it in this world. She has every thing under control. She has every thing under control, except the traffic!

As Ann leaves her office, she glances at her watch. "One hour and five minutes until I pick up the kids at soccer practice." Ann settles into the cockpit of the new red BMW she received from James for her birthday. As she starts the engine, she enjoys its throaty hum. The musky smell of the leather seats reminds her of the marketplace she loves to visit when she and James go on vacation to Mexico. And the air conditioner blowing cool air on her face takes the edge off a hot, humid central Texas day. She slips in her favorite CD and prepares for the hour drive home.

Backing out of her parking place, Ann notices a car coming toward her. She pauses, smiles, and waves the other car on. Exiting from the parking garage, she turns right and drives two blocks to a stop sign.

Ann is sweet, kind, and helpful. She arrives at the stop sign about the same time as the car on her right. She smiles and motions the other driver on.

Five more blocks and she's at the entrance to I-35. Ann's philosophy about driving the freeway is almost biblical: "Go forth and they shall make room for you."

Ann charges onto the freeway, forcing the car behind her to abruptly slow, which causes many other cars in that lane to suddenly slow down. Needless to say, if any vehicles in that lane had been trucks, there would be no sudden slowing. Ann, the sweet person who waves on others at stop signs, has made her first strike.

A few miles and the scenery changes. Ann is now on the edge of the city. She makes her move to save time by jumping from the freeway to the frontage road, then forces her way back onto the freeway when the frontage road traffic increases.

Because the freeway is under construction, the exit ramps are shorter than normal. As Ann nears an exit ramp, she glances over her right shoulder to determine the amount of traffic on the frontage road. If she thinks she can go faster on the frontage road, she will slow abruptly to reduce her speed to exit the freeway.

Know what happens to the people behind her? Abrupt slowing, but we know a truck isn't capable of abrupt slowing.

Ann creates another safety hazard for the professional driver.

Exit and enter, exit and enter. She has children to pick up at soccer practice. She has shopping to do. She has clothes to pick up at the dry cleaners. She has her schedule to make.

Exit and enter, exit and enter, until she gets to her neighborhood.

Ann enjoys the hum of her red BMW, the musky smell of the leather seats, and she must tell James how the air conditioner takes the edge off a hot, humid central Texas day. She sings along with her favorite CD. Then sweet Ann smiles and waves other people on at the stop sign near her house.

Ann, the person who waves on others at stop signs, has her schedule and you better not get in her way. Ann has everything under control.

How do nice people like Ann get to be so aggressive on the road? Some safety experts think it is learned from childhood. Many children are reared in a culture where irate behavior is part of their parents' way of driving. In the car, many of the rules of behavior change. The parents demonstrate that it is okay to be mad, upset, out of control and, yes, use of foul language is acceptable in this scenario.

By the time children reach driving age, they have observed years of road rage.

This negative behavior can be unlearned, but like any bad behavior, before it can be changed, the person doing the bad behavior must want to change. Then, after deciding to change, the person must work hard to change. And like any bad habit, people sometimes fall back into their old ways.

Additionally, it appears there are some drivers who do not want to change. So, unfortunately, there are a lot of aggressive drivers out there.

How does aggressive driving turn into road rage? According to Leon James and Diane Nahl in their *Aggressive Driving Prevention for Law Enforcement*, aggressive driving is defined as driving under the influence of impaired emotions.

Additionally, James and Nahl stated that there are three categories of impaired emotions and each type of impaired emotions leads to a specific type of dangerous driving. The three categories of impaired emotions are:

1. Impatience and inattentiveness

2. Power struggle

3. Recklessness and road rage

Each category of impaired emotions leads to different types of traffic violations. The categories and their associated traffic violations are listed below.

Category 1: Impatience and Inattentiveness

Driving through red traffic lights

Speeding up to make it though a yellow traffic light

Rolling stops

Cutting corners or rolling over double lines

Blocking intersections

Not yielding

Improper lane changes or weaving

Driving 5 to 15 mph above the limit

Following too close

Not signaling when required

Erratically slowing down or speeding up

Category 2: Power Struggle

Blocking passing lane; refusing to move over

Threatening or insulting by yelling, gesturing, or honking repeatedly

Tailgating to punish or coerce

Cutting off another driver at intersection, lane change, or the like

Braking suddenly to retaliate

Category 3: Recklessness and Road Rage

Driving drunk

Pointing a gun or shooting

Assaulting with the car or using it as a battering object

Driving at very high speeds

Anatomy of a Road Rage Tragedy

Let's look at a simple scenario to see how a typical incident can escalate from aggression to road rage.

When an incident happens between two drivers, one or both drivers may experience some anger. At this point, the drivers can go their separate ways and the incident will be over.

Another choice, unfortunately, is for one or both of the drivers to continue the aggressive behavior. When the drivers continue their aggressive behavior, they become angrier and angrier until the anger turns into rage. The longer the cycle of exchanges between the drivers goes on, the more intense the feelings become and the drivers are less inclined to back down.

Incidents that evolve into road rage happen in steps. At each step, the persons involved have a choice to accelerate their hostilities or end it. If you look at these steps and the choices the persons have, you can understand how road rage develops.

The following information of an incident of road rage was given in written testimony to the U.S. House Subcommittee on Transportation and Infrastructure by Dr Leon James, professor of psychology at the University of Hawaii.

The incident, which occurred in Cincinnati, involved a 24-year-old mother of two and a pregnant woman. The sequence of events was reconstructed from a Court TV broadcast case where the 24-year-old was the defendant in a criminal suit for road rage.

Sequence of Road Rage Steps

Step 1: A 24-year-old mother of two, alone in a GrandAm (GA), is following a VW. In front of them are several cars behind a truck going 35 mph. The GA pulls into the left lane to pass and speeds up to 55 mph.

Step 2: The VW, going 20 mph slower than the GA, suddenly pulls into the lane in front of the GA and forces it to apply the brakes.

Choice Points

Choice 1: Overtaking a line of vehicles is always risky. Expect others to change lanes. Restrain yourself and accommodate others.

Choice 2: Avoid engaging in power struggles with other drivers. It takes skill to back down from a challenge. It is best to be less competitive and not get

Step 3: The VW gradually overtakes the slow truck, passes it, and pulls back into the right lane.

Step 4: The GA, still in the left lane, overtakes the VW, honks several times, makes obscene gestures, and flashes the lights as signs of outrage (the GA driver later said, "to let her know that she almost caused an accident").

Step 5: The VW driver responds by flipping the GA driver the bird and shaking her head.

Step 6: The GA now tries to pull ahead in the left lane in order to reenter the right lane, but the VW accelerates, blocking the way.

Step 7: The GA slows down and pulls in behind the VW, but

Choice 2: *(continued)* involved with other drivers in some negative way.

Choice 3: The GA driver at this point should show self-control by letting the VW go on its way.

Choice 4: One of the worst things a driver can do is openly duel with another driver. The GA driver used all of the behaviors known to be acts of war on the road. What the GA driver should have done was practice self-control by resisting the temptation to teach other drivers a lesson. Valuing the VW driver as another human being would have given the GA driver the inner power to resist the impulse to retaliate.

Choice 5: The worst thing to do in a road rage power struggle is to continue the duel. The VW driver should not have responded in any manner.

Choice 6: Escalation by both drivers leads to more rage. Both drivers are locking themselves into a no-win situation. Both drivers at this point need to back off. But it is hard to do so after both have engaged in this "battle of the egos."

Choice 7: This lull in the event could be used by both drivers as

Step 7: *(continued)* keeps up the pressure by tailgating dangerously.

Step 8: Now the GA suddenly pulls out into the left lane again, overtakes, and cuts off the VW, then gives the VW driver a "brake job" to punish her.

Step 9: The VW driver applies her brakes suddenly and they lock, causing her to veer sideways to the right where she hits a truck parked on the side of the road. She is thrown from the car and taken to the hospital where she recovers from surgery, but her unborn child dies.

Step 10: The GA driver continues her trip to the work site where she told her supervisor that she had been in an accident, that "the other driver had it coming," and that "she wasn't going to take **** from no one." Later, she was arrested and charged with vehicular homicide for causing the death of the unborn child.

Choice 7: *(continued)* a time to calm down. Drivers need to learn how to back out of a fight by practicing "an attitude of latitude" or forgiveness.

Choice 8: The GA driver is clearly the aggressor now. The GA driver, who got upset because the VW driver almost caused an accident in Step 2, is now creating a major battle. Her only hope of being a safe driver is at some time in the future to completely overhaul her aggressive driving personality and driving philosophy.

Choice 9: The VW driver nearly caused a crash by pulling out in front of the GA. Instead of backing off her aggressive behavior, she flipped the GA driver the bird, and ended up losing her baby. There are no choices to be made at this point. It has gone too far.

Choice 10: The GA driver not only had no remorse, but also was proud of what she did and bragged about it. This came back to haunt her when it was brought out at the trial through the testimony of her supervisor. Both drivers need driver personality makeovers that will involve examining and changing their self-image, their ego relationships with cars, their values about human rights, their anger management, and their caring about fellow human beings.

The trial of the GA driver took place in Cincinnati in 1997. The GA driver was found guilty of aggravated vehicular homicide and aggravated assault. The GA driver was sentenced to a one-and-a-half-year prison term. What can a professional driver learn from this? A review of the choice points is a good starting place.

Review of Choice Points

Overtaking a line of vehicles is always risky.

Expect others to change lanes.

Restrain yourself and accommodate others.

Avoid engaging in power struggles.

It takes skill to back down.

Don't be competitive with other drivers.

Show self-control.

Don't duel with other drivers.

Resist the temptation to teach other drivers a lesson.

Value other drivers as human beings.

Resist the impulse to retaliate.

Don't escalate the situation.

If involved in an incident, use a lull in events to calm down.

Practice an "attitude of latitude" or forgiveness.

If you look at the Review of Choice Points list, you will see that all the points on the list can be divided into two categories. The first is the use of safe driving practices, such as not overtaking other vehicles, and expecting other drivers to change lanes. The rest of the points have to do with drivers' emotions and attitudes regarding other persons.

In driving school, professional drivers are taught safe driving practices. Many companies have training classes where safe driving practices are discussed. And there are posters in break rooms and spots on TV regarding safe driving practices.

But it was the drivers' attitude and emotions that caused the above incident. Remember Point 10? It stated that both drivers needed personality makeovers, which will involve examining and changing their self-images, their values about human rights, their anger management styles, and their caring about fellow human beings.

If road rage is caused by drivers' poor self-image, lack of value of human rights, anger, and lack of caring about fellow human beings, what in the world can be done to change all of these aggressive drivers?

We currently get some education regarding self-image, human rights, anger control, and care about fellow human beings at school, in after-school activities such as band, drama, debate, and sports, some at home from our parents, and some at church. But is what we are doing now making a drastic reduction in the number of aggressive drivers? Let's do a quick review of the data.

As stated earlier in this chapter: Ricardo Martinez, federal administrator of NHTSA, declared that road rage is now the number-one traffic problem. The *New York Times* reported a poll showing that 42% of the residents rate aggressive drivers as the biggest threat on the road, The AAA Foundation for Traffic Safety released data in 1996 showing that the average number of violent incidents reported among drivers in the U.S. has increased annually over the past eight years, 51% since 1990.

Many safety experts believe that, for every act of aggressive driving reported to the police or reported in the newspapers, there are hundreds or thousands more that never get reported.

Hundreds or thousands that never get reported! And you as a professional driver are out there every day trying to make a living and avoid those "crazy people."

It appears that the number of aggressive drivers is not going down; in fact, according to the data, the number is increasing. If what we are doing now is not reducing the number of aggressive drivers, what can be done?

Many safety experts think aggressive driving is a cultural trait. That is to say, that we learn from our parents, from school, from TV, from video games, and from movies that it okay to be aggressive, to be angry, to not care about the rights of others, and not care about fellow human beings. Many of the actions of family members and schools activities cause children to develop a poor self-image.

To change a cultural trait requires the concentrated efforts of all the institutions of a society. We have to attack the driving rage problem similar to the way we, as a nation, attacked the problem of tobacco use. National, state, and local governments will have to have a role. All levels of educational institutions will have to have a role. Television, the movies, and video games will have to have a role. Only this type of approach will have the power and authority to convince millions of drivers to change their driving styles and reactions to other drivers' styles of driving.

What is Being Done Now?

Unfortunately for the professional driver, the person probably most subjected to road rage, there is not a lot being done. Many of our governmental agencies are at the level where they have recognized the problem and are developing programs to address it. It doesn't appear that the entertainment industry, the movies, TV, or video games are doing much about the problem. Many schools are teaching children how to manage their anger, how to peacefully resolve conflicts, to have respect for others, and help children develop positive self-images.

Some grass-roots groups are being developed to address the problem of road rage. And some church groups and some social/service organizations such as the Lions, Rotary, and the Junior Chamber of Commerce have programs to address the problem. Dr. James has started small groups called Quality Driving Circles (QDC) where the individual members carry small tape recorders to record their thoughts as they drive. These tapes, which are shared at the QDC meetings, are called self-witnessing reports. These reports include the drivers thoughts and feelings while they are behind the wheel, a driving personality makeover project, and such things as checklists, tests, and inventories to help keep track of patterns of driving behaviors.

Through his work with Quality Driving Circles, Dr. James has developed a profile of safe drivers, which he calls "Smart Drivers." While aggressive drivers are dangerous, antisocial, and intolerant, Smart Drivers have the following characteristics:

Characteristics of Smart Drivers

Supportive of other drivers

Rational in their actions

Have emotional control skills

Accommodate rather than oppose other drivers

Have developed a positive self-image

Value others' rights

Care about other human beings

So there are programs being developed and implemented to stop aggressive driving. These programs will have to focus on the current 180 million drivers and on the next generation of drivers. External methods of dealing with aggressive driving such as road improvement, automobile safety engineering, safety regulations, law enforcement, information campaigns, and traditional driver education programs are all helpful but according to Dr. James and many other safety experts, major changes in the reduction of road rage must come through changing the culture of hostility on the road.

What can a professional driver do about the problem of aggressive drivers? The authors of this chapter asked that question of several drivers one cold winter day at a truck stop in Ohio. One of the many who had some good suggestions was Juan Cortez.

Juan, a local driver, who works about 10 hours a day making deliveries in a large midwestern city, told us about some his experiences.

"Since I do most of my driving in the city, I have more intersections and traffic lights to deal with than the guys who drive on the interstates. My biggest problem day in and day out comes from what I think you called the impatient and inattentive drivers.

"You got to really watch out for those impatient dudes. They will drive right through a red light or speed up when they see a yellow. And they think a stop sign means go right on though. You got to really look at every intersection. Just because you have the right of way doesn't mean some dude's going to yield. And those guys who blink their lights, honk their horns, and change lanes real fast are dangerous. You never know what one of those dudes might do. When I see one of those dudes in my rearview mirror coming up behind me real fast, I get in the right lane and slow down a little bit. You got to give those guys lots of space to do their thing.

"And those inattentive drivers," said Juan. "They are in a world of their own. If you see someone driving and talking on a phone, watch out. They might do anything. And those people driving along and looking for the address of some building, they weave all over the road and make sudden lane changes or turns. You can see their little brain working, 'Oops, there's what I am looking for,' as they cut across two lanes of traffic.

"And I'll tell you another thing I learned. You can't tell how a person will drive by how they are dressed or what kind of car they drive. When I first started driving, if some doll would pass me who was dressed fine and I could smell her perfume as she passed, I would think among other things, she was cool and had it all together. Or if I saw some guy in a big car with a beard and glasses, I would think that guy must be a doctor or lawyer or something like that. It didn't take me long to find out those type of people sometimes do stupid things just like anyone else. You got to look out for everyone.

"So I see lots of those impatient and inattentive drivers, and my share of power struggles that lead to aggression and then to road rage. What do I do about that power struggle and road rage stuff? I keep my cool and let them go on their way. If I see a driver acting aggressive toward me, I wave at them, say I am sorry, and put plenty of distance between them and me.

"I have a job that I like. I have a family that I love and they love me. I have two sons that I need to show how to catch a cat-fish and how to throw a football. I have a little daughter who is smart as a whip and I'm encouraging her to be president of the United States. I exercise and eat right. I have a great life and I am not going to jeopardize it by getting into it with some fool on the road.

"If someone gets aggressive towards me, I smile, I say 'I'm sorry,' I put some distance between me and the crazy driver, and I let them go on down the road. I don't involved with crazy people!"

Juan seems to have everything figured out while he's on the road. And if he follows his own advice, he may even have a chance to see his daughter become president of the United States.

ONE MORE MEETING WITH A PROFESSIONAL DRIVER

The authors wanted to run this information past one more truck driver. We met our friend Bob from the beginning of this chapter, one hot, humid summer day at Dorsett's 221 Restaurant near Buda. After we talked with Bob about this chapter, Bob said, "Let me tell you what it means to me."

"There are crazy drivers out there on the road! Heavy traffic and construction on the highway make them crazier. Some of them may be crazy drivers because their parents were crazy drivers.

"If we are going to have fewer of these crazy drivers on the road, we will have to teach kids through the home, through church, and through sports and things like that to have a posi-tive self-image, how to deal with anger, and how to care about and respect others.

"For the crazy drivers now driving, we need a nationwide ef-fort such as the stop-smoking program to help them develop a better self-image, to better deal with anger, and convince them to care about and respect other drivers.

"For me, personally, I kind of like what Juan said. I also have a great family who loves me and I love them. My kids and I are going to start our own trucking company after they graduate from college. I'm eating better, walking some, losing some weight, and sleeping better. For a good old boy from south Louisiana, I have a pretty good life and I am not going to let some crazy driver screw it up.

"As for me, I am going to wave at them, say 'I'm sorry' as often as I need to, put a lot of space between them and me, and not get involved with a crazy four-wheeler.

"I'll keep my cool and keep my distance."

You got it Bob. I'll see you on down the road!

Chapter 11

Resolving Conflicts at Work and at Home

TAKE COMPLAINTS SERIOUSLY

Imagine someone promising to do something, then completely ignoring that promise. If you were the person who was promised something, and the other person broke his or her promise, you probably wouldn't feel too positive about that person.

Now, think of a purchase you made recently. You got it home, used it for about 30 minutes, and then it quit working or didn't work when you really needed it.

Think of a service company—a plumbing company in this example—that charges you for unclogging your sink, and then you find they only did half the job or didn't do the job at all.

Does any of this sound familiar?

Sadly, one or all of these situations are all too familiar to every one of us. And what is our usual reaction? Of course, we're angry or disappointed, but usually angry first.

Anger is one of our most powerful emotions, an emotion that's more contagious than kindness. Translated, this means if you're angry, chances are the person you're speaking with will soon be angry, too.

Of course, it doesn't always happen like this, but for some of us, the anger we experience because of a broken promise, a defective product, or a cancelled trip soon becomes our total focus. And what good does it do? It soon leads to confusion and we—at least for an instant—don't want to focus on finding a solution. Instead, we choose to focus on our anger and spew it over anyone brave enough to stand within range.

Okay, here's Lesson #1: When you are dealing with an angry customer, it is best to focus on the facts, then give him the options. For example, take the situation Martha Green found herself in when she arrived at the dock at the appointed time, only to find the shipment wasn't ready for loading. After calling the dispatcher, Martha sat in the waiting area and fumed.

Tonight of all nights she wanted to be home on time because her daughter's second grade class was presenting the program at the 7:30 p.m. PTA meeting. She had missed other school events, but she thought this would be no problem since the middle of the week wasn't usually as busy as Mondays and Fridays.

The dispatcher said he didn't have any more pickups, so she could wait at the shipper's office or come back later. Neither choice made her too happy, and she was careful not to say anything to the shipper.

Note: People who are angry often get angrier as they feel more disappointment. A good way to help them regain control of their emotions is to focus on the facts. Bottom line, you'll be less stressed and the customer will be happier with the outcome.

The dock foreman came in, offered her a Coke, and when Martha refused, sat down. "I don't want to be here overtime any more than you do so we'll get you loaded as soon as they start packaging those pallets," he offered.

Martha thanked him and explained she was trying to punch out in time to make it to a school program. Martha did make it home and to the school program on time, but her anger had exhausted her to the point that she was not able to truly enjoy seeing her daughter perform.

The shipper could have tried the following, easy, four-step approach with Martha when he found she was upset:

1. First, tell them you are sorry about the problem and thank them for bringing the problem to you attention if they have done so.

2. Tell them you understand why this isn't a comfortable situation for them.

3. Listen to what they tell you and then assure the customer you'll do everything possible to fix the situation.

4. Then, do something.

In this case, once the foreman had talked with Martha, he excused himself and went back to the packing department so he could personally oversee the progress on the shipment she was waiting for. A few times during the process, he stepped back into the waiting room to let Martha know that progress was being made.

Another note: Irate persons will respond more positively when they know you've taken their complaint seriously. And remember, you don't know what good service is until you don't get it.

DON'T TAKE THE COMPLAINT PERSONALLY? YEAH, SURE!

Have you ever heard a salesperson say he didn't take it personally when someone didn't buy from him?

One of this country's well-known sales gurus makes a good argument against this ages-old suggestion: Not to take it personally when a customer turns you down. "Most sales professionals explain, they're not turning you down: they just don't want to buy your product," the guru said. "But, this is bad advice. They're flat wrong!

The guru goes on: "I'd take it personally if someone turned down my product! Why? Because the turn-down *is* going to affect me personally. It's going to affect *my* quota. It's going to affect my total sales for the week and it's darned sure going to affect my commission check," he said. "Now that's pretty *personal* in my book!"

So, what happens when a customer—shipper or consignee—spews angry words at you? Do you take it personally?

John drove his bobtail up to the dock at AAA Consolidated for a pickup. He walked into the customer's office to pick up the paperwork. "Oh, man. Did anyone at your company teach you guys how to drive? The last idiot you sent over tore up my rails. You be sure you aren't the same idiot. And keep your eyes open while you're in this yard!"

Experts tell us that not taking the "spew" personally requires a lot of discipline, and these skills have to be learned and relearned because it is not easy to change. It takes plenty of practice to let these complaints bounce off.

There's one other important point to make here: once customers become angry with a carrier or a driver, they don't hesitate to share their anger with others. One study found that one unhappy customer will share his or her complaints against you and/or your company with as many as 20 other people.

Studies also show that 90 percent of unhappy customers never complain. And, customers that do complain—and have their problem solved quickly and fairly—are usually more satisfied than customers who never have a problem.

Of course, John probably isn't the cause of the shipper's problem, but he doesn't think of things in this way. And the shipper probably doesn't really care if John is the cause or not. All he wants is for someone representing your company to hear him and have the problem resolved quickly.

Since John was the unlucky driver to show up at the shipper's dock today, he's the one who has to handle the situation. Strangely, as long as your customer has a problem, your firm has a problem, too.

So, here's the picture. The shipper is upset because of damage to his dock caused by one of John's fellow drivers. Here's what John should do:

1. When someone has a complaint, give him or her your undivided attention.

2. This undivided attention gives you an opportunity to reestablish the reputation of your company and may be enough to keep the shipper from calling your competitor for the next shipment.

3. A customer complaint gives your management an opportunity to take a closer look at the service your company is giving, day in and day out. This may also give them an opportunity to head off a much larger crisis.

STEPS TOWARD RESOLVING A CONFLICT

When customers jump on your case when you arrive at their dock or place of business, they are often angry, sometimes really angry. They are also emotional and probably not too rational. The important thing is not to allow yourself to be sucked into their emotional hailstorm.

Remember, you're there to do a job. You're there to help the shippers get their loads to their customers in good shape and on time. Getting angry at the customer makes your job impossible if you really want to help.

By the time you roll up to the dock, the angry shipper has probably been angry at two or three other people, and called your terminal, reaming out several employees for the damage one of the other drivers did to the dock. The customer is angry, confused, and irrational at this point. He feels some pain about this situation or wouldn't have jumped your case in the first place. Now the customer is also feeling frustration because the damage wasn't repaired on his timetable, which was immediately.

Want your customer to get over this anger? Try this.

1. Listen and understand the problem.

2. Let him know you've heard the complaint and you understand.

3. Act on the complaint. Either make a phone call to the terminal for an update from the dispatcher or let someone know after you've picked up the load.

Next, after your customer rants and raves, be sure he knows how much you and your company value his trust and his business. Let him know you understand the cause of this distress and the frustration he must feel about the situation.

Finally, reassure the customer. Be empathetic about the situation. Empathy means putting yourself in the customer's place and thinking about how you would feel in the same situation.

Sometimes, the irate customer may just want an acknowledgement from the highest management personnel in your firm. It isn't always easy to know exactly what this person wants, but your job is to be positive, be reassuring, and not get into a shouting match or argument.

Some carriers have written procedures for handling many common or recurring customer problems. At Disneyland, for example, employees have a policy manual of written procedures for handling many problems, including helping visitors find their lost car because parking lots at the entertainment center are so massive.

Mahatma Ghandi once said,

"A customer is the most important visitor on our premises. He is not dependent on us. We are dependent on him. He is not interrupting our work. He is the purpose for it. He is not an outsider in our business. He is part of it. We are not doing him a favor by serving him. He is doing us a favor by giving us the opportunity to do so."

WIN-WIN CUSTOMER SERVICE IS A NO-BRAINER

You've probably heard about win-win customer service before. It works this way: you solve the problem and salvage the company's reputation with that customer. The customer gets satisfaction through the solution you offer, and the relationship between the customer and the firm is left with little or no lasting damage.

There are also several other outcomes possible when an angry customer hits you with a complaint.

There's the *I Lose—You Win* outcome, where the company may lose a substantial amount of money without any benefit from solving the customer's problem a certain way.

There's the *I Lose—You Lose* outcome where you become angry with the customer, the customer becomes angrier, and you lose his business.

Getting to *I Win—You Win* requires more than sweet-talking a customer. Once you've calmed him down, you or your company must be able to offer a solution. Then say, "Here's what will happen next." Then, review the step-by-step way you plan to solve the problem. Then ask, "Does this meet with your approval?" If the customer answers "No!" ask what else you can do to arrive at a happy end.

LISTEN, ACKNOWLEDGE, ACT

When you are confronted with irate customers, you have to understand what's really happening when there's a problem. First of all, they want some personalized attention. If they haven't gotten it through calling your terminal or your boss, they're looking for it from you.

This customer obviously wants you—someone, anyone—to listen to his tale of woe. He wants attention and he wants it now. Listening is an important skill and a critical skill in resolving any conflict or problem.

If you don't take the time to listen—and really listen—to this customer and his problem, you've missed an opportunity to help. Don't be filling out paperwork. Don't be eating a snack. Really listen!

1. Listen and respond appropriately. Don't just say "uh-huh" after every sentence.

2. Have the customer clarify any fact or any sequence of events you don't understand. This clarification will also give you some hints about what it will take to please this customer, to solve the problem or satisfy the complaint.

3. Don't make this mistake (which is made often): Don't let a customer's anger keep you from hearing the problem and what he needs to be satisfied. It's entirely human nature to get caught up in the emotion, but try to keep your eyes on the facts and only the facts. If you ever try to deal with an angry customer without finding out the facts, there's *no way* you'll ever find a solution to the problem.

Acknowledge the customer and the complaint. No, you don't know exactly how he or she feels and don't fall into the trap of saying you do *because you don't!* Instead, tell your customer you're sorry and understand how this situation has caused some inconvenience or whatever is appropriate for the situation.

When the customer feels you've heard and understood the problem by what you say as an acknowledgement, he or she can begin to focus less on the anger and more on finding a mutual solution.

And make sure the customer hears your acknowledgement. Sometimes, he is so angry and irrational that he may not be listening, so it doesn't hurt to say, "I'm sorry" or "I understand how this may have inconvenienced you" several times. This assures the customer has heard what you've said.

Now that you've listened, you've heard the complaint, and you've acknowledged this to the customer, it's time for you or your company to decide what to do about the problem. This may be as simple as re-assuring the customer that someone will be there to fix the dock or it may require a visit from the terminal manager. If you or your company acknowledge the customer's problem and then do nothing about it, this will cause an even bigger problem.

Some folks think offering an apology is the same thing as taking action. It isn't. If you apologize and then don't take any action, it's like offering someone you love a beautifully wrapped gift box with nothing inside.

So, what action should be taken? Well, it is possible your company won't be able to do exactly what the customer wants. Remember, this isn't a perfect world. But, also understand that the key to a customer's satisfaction is a relatively quick and fair solution that your company will get to work on immediately.

Your firm can spend thousands of dollars on advertising. You can tell your customers anything, but your actions are the only things that really count. The message here is: "Make sure your actions match your advertising claims."

CRISIS MANAGEMENT—SOMETIMES A REAL PAIN

While we don't have space to go into all the steps involved in managing a crisis here, there are some similarities between a crisis and an incident that creates a customer complaint. In a few of these cases, an incident could escalate into a crisis, but this is rare. And escalation is rarer still if your firm tries to provide an immediate solution to the customer's problem.

When people talk about crisis management today, they'll usually remember the Tylenol tampering case from a decade ago to make their point. For those who don't remember the case, it occurred in a metropolitan area when someone put poison in bottles of Tylenol and at least one death occurred as a result.

Tylenol's parent company stepped up to the microphones of the media and said the company was aware of the problem, and had recalled all Tylenol from store shelves and customers until they had all been inspected. Once the inspection was completed and no further evidence of tampering had been found, Tylenol spearheaded a movement to make it more difficult for people to tamper with drugs by using advanced packaging.

By acknowledging the problem to the public, the makers of Tylenol achieved two goals: they made the public more trusting of the company and made it difficult for competing companies to create media campaigns against Tylenol.

Acknowledging the problem doesn't mean apologizing and accepting the blame for the problem. Acknowledgement just lets the public know you realize the situation and are working to solve the problem.

SOME FINAL THOUGHTS

Whenever you are confronted with an irate customer, a complaint or a crisis, remember the following.

1. Understand there will be complaints, and that some customers will be highly emotional when they confront you or your company with their problem.

2. Don't think the customer's complaint is the end of the world. It isn't. Try to keep it at a business level rather than a personal one.

3. Listen, listen, listen. Good service means letting the customer spew. Then help him or her refocus on the facts of the situation and outline what is expected of your company.

4. Look for ways to solve the problem that are going to be well received by the customer and don't compromise your company's policies.

5. Be aware that the speedy resolution of the problem will promote the greatest good will for your company. One CEO said, "Some of our best processes and policies have come as a result of complaints from our customers."

6. Be empathetic.

7. The firm's reputation will be less damaged—and perhaps it will be strengthened—if the problem is solved and the customer is satisfied.

8. If a problematic situation becomes a crisis, develop a strategy and acknowledge the crisis immediately to the community and the media.

9. Be careful and don't over-react, making every problem a crisis.

10. Learn from every complaint. Keep honing your skills on dealing with problems and difficult people. As one professional guru reminds, "I've been in this business for 20 years and have learned that the only things I can count on are problems, and change."

Chapter 12

Reassurance:
It's a Two-Way Street

If you have ever worked for a boss who never let you know where you stood, you know stress and frustration. In some cases, the frustration grows to the point of exploding and creates a perfect time to exit the job. . . . And this very uncomfortable relationship.

But what if that boss took time each day to tell you what a good job you were doing or how much he or she appreciated your professionalism? What if your boss took you aside from time to time and praised you for your strengths and gave you pointers on how to improve the job you were doing?

Everyone craves this type of reassurance. It's a basic human need.

Similarly, your friends and family could use the same kind of reassurance (not about the job they're doing, of course). But,they could use some encouraging words from you, like how much you miss them when you're away from home, how much you love them, and how much you appreciate everything they do to keep the home fires burning.

Okay, okay. Some of you may already be saying, "Hey, don't I let them know how important they are to me by getting into that cab, day in and day out . . . by driving thousands of miles every year . . . and bringing home a paycheck every week?"

And the answer to your question is, "Of course you do, but sometimes the people at home—while you're gone every week or while you're gone every three weeks—could use some simple reassurance.

Relationship specialists speaking about maintaining healthy, romantic relationships with significant others, provide these suggestions.

1. *Never* take each other for granted and appreciate everything you do for each other. That lets both of you know that you are wanted and needed. And there's nothing wrong about saying "thank you" and "I love you" several times every day because it helps you love each other better.

2. Don't stay angry or annoyed at each other. Why? Because time goes by that you could be loving each other instead of finding fault with each other.

3. The happier you are outside your life together, the happier your life together will be. This is especially important when both of you work outside the home.

4. The most important parts of a relationship are trust and communication.

5. Love your partner or your friends with all your heart, every second of every day, and *make sure they know it.*

6. Don't pay attention to what other people have to say about your relationship because the only thing that truly matters is how the two of you feel. If you are shallow enough to let someone else's opinion become more important than your own, the relationship is over before it ever began.

In every case and in every relationship, taking time to reassure your partner or your family or friends is time worth taking. Because each of us is different, everyone has different needs. Some need more communication than others. Others need to be held close more often. But because we are humans, each of us needs reassurance about how we are valued, how much room there is for us in another's life, how much opportunity we may have with a particular company, or how we feel about that individual.

As you read through this chapter, think about ways reassurance can make a difference in your life and in the lives of those people who are important to you.

MEET DANNY AND SHERRY

They had been married for almost two years when Danny took a job that kept him over-the-road for two weeks at a time. "The money was too good," Danny would say later, "much more than I could make working at the lumberyard in town.

When Danny went over-the-road, Sherry remembered it as a type of abandonment. "I knew we would be talking every day or two, but all of a sudden, I was responsible for every single thing that happened at our home," she said. "Thank God, my folks lived about two miles from us and my dad could help when I didn't know what to do when the water heater flooded the garage or the car needed a new transmission."

Donna, a woman Sherry met at a truckers' spouse support group at Danny's company, told the group one night about how it had been when her husband Dick first went on the road. "Every little thing that happened that I couldn't take care of became a very big deal," she said. "I let little things esca-late into big deals, so when Dick came in, I was a mess. I was angry, defeated, and just in a heap. Eventually, whatever prob-lem had caused me to crumble was solved, but not before I had made a complete idiot out of myself."

Donna found that several women in the group had experi-enced the same kind of panic when something went wrong while their husbands were gone. "A better approach to these problems," she said calmly, "is to sit back, figure out what your options are, figure out the best or the most affordable way of handling it yourself, and skip the panic. Or, as they say on TV, 'save the drama for your mama.'"

Sherry soon learned that she and Danny could enjoy themselves more while he was home if she solved many of the problems before he hit the door. "At first, every time he came in, there was a problem," she admitted.

"Yeah, and I found myself sorta dreading getting back to town because I knew there was something screwed up even before I pulled in the gate," Danny admitted.

"Guess I've gone from, 'Help! Help!' to 'I took care of it honey,'" Sherry said. "And, when he gets home, I don't meet him at the door with a crisis."

But Danny knows that Sherry needs recognition for her growth and her willingness to handle the situations when they arise, even if she's had no experience with central heat or plumbing or a broken pipe. "Every time we talk when I'm away from home, I tell her how good she does things," Danny said, "and I let her know how much I love her."

Sherry is also aware that this reassurance from her husband goes a long way and she is sure to give Danny reassurance, too. "I've been on the road with him," she said. "I know he works hard and I know he gets lonely, so I make sure I tell him how much I love him and how much I appreciate how hard he's working. We're saving to have a family some day and to get a bigger house, so he's doing everything he does for us, and I try to do my part at home with my job at the bank and by taking care of our home while he's away."

For both Danny and Sherry, providing reassurance to each other keeps their relationship strong and their goals in sharp focus. And both say they don't hesitate to thank the other for the contribution each is making to their soon-to-be family.

WHAT KAREN AND BRAD NEEDED

Unlike Danny and Sherry, Karen and Brad had been married for 15 years, and Brad had been over the road for most of that time. Karen admits that it was tough at first, having her husband away from home for three or four weeks at a time, but with her job and, later, their two children, she had plenty to keep herself busy.

> "The kids take a lot of my time, especially now since they're involved in school activities and sports," Karen said. "I take them to practices, and go to their games and their programs at school, so we have a pretty full schedule every day. But I also found that I needed to spend some time to take care of me, so I started identifying what I needed to keep going while Brad was on the road."

> Karen often takes a few hours over the weekend to get her hair done, or she may drop into the beauty salon for a manicure and pedicure. "It may be selfish, but if Brad were here, he'd insist that I get a few hours to myself," she said. "Sometimes, the kids and I will just go to the park, and while they're playing, I'll take a book with me and enjoy being outside while I read."

> Brad has nothing but praise for Karen, and he's not shy about giving it to her when they're together or in a group. "I'm real lucky," Brad said. "My wife keeps everything going while I'm gone, she's raising the kids and still looks great. I can't wait to get home after a trip."

> Karen is also good about reassuring Brad about their relationship, even after 15 years. "I think it's important to keep as much of the romance we once had as possible, so I really look for ways for us to have 'our time,' once the kids are in bed. Or, whenever its convenient, the kids will go over to their grandparents' house to spend one night so Brad and I can have some peace and quiet."

Karen likes to do at least one thing to rekindle their romance when Brad's at home, and here are some of her ideas.

1. Arrange a date night and you plan the date.

2. Share a sunset together or get up early enough to watch the sun rise. Hold hands as you both experience the moment.

3. Plan a picnic and find a secluded picnic spot so you can be "really alone."

4. Go skinny dipping where it's safe. In Karen and Brad's case, Karen's sister has a pool in her backyard, so they 'borrow' it when her sister's family is out of town.

5. Feed each other strawberries dipped in chocolate.

6. Buy some scented lotion or oil, and give each other a back rub or a massage.

7. Take a walk in the country. The exercise will create endorphins that will make both of you feel great.

8. Pick out a restaurant neither of you has visited before and have fun exploring the new experience.

9. Rent a DVD or video, put the kids to bed, and have a picnic on the floor of your den or living room, and watch the movie.

10. Don't let 24 hours pass without letting the other know how much you love them and how much they mean to you.

Whether Karen and Brad realize it or not, all of the special things they do together are ways of reassuring each other. The time they spend—together and as a family—reinforces their shared goals. Their conversations, their walks, and time quiet times they spend reassure each other that they are on the right road.

When the kids graduate, Karen plans to go on the road with Brad. They tried it for three weeks last summer and Karen loved it. And, if all goes well, she's going to get her CDL so she can do some of the driving. "It'll be good for both of us, and besides, we deserve more time together," they agreed.

REASSURING THE KIDS

Tommy came in one day, his face dirty and his shirt ripped. When questioned by his mother, he told her he had gotten into a fight when he got off the bus. "One of the kids told me I didn't have a daddy, so I whopped him," Tommy reported.

It isn't unusual when dad's over-the-road that the kids may get questions about where their dad is or why he wasn't at the last swim meet.

In this day and age, where families have been separated, mixed with second marriages, and where single parents are often more the rule than the exception, kids have a lot more leeway than they once did. But reassurance from both parents is still very important.

"As soon as the kids were old enough to talk on the phone, we made sure Glen spoke to each of them every time he called," said Mary. "And, of course, when he's home, he takes time to spend a few hours with each of them, separately."

These one-on-ones with the absent parent reassures the child that they are, indeed, important and their thoughts and stories of what they've been doing while mom or dad is away are worth taking time to hear. "My time is one of the gifts I can give my kids when I'm home," said Glen. "And I make sure I have time to spend with them and with my wife whenever I'm not in the truck."

Glen's company has a fairly liberal riders' policy, so each summer since both kids have been in school, the entire family goes on the road, visiting interesting destinations between dropping and picking up loads. "It's good for all of us," Mary said. "We all get to see what Glen does while he's away from us, and the kids have questions they can ask when we're back at home and he goes out again. They're learning the business, you might say."

Last summer, they visited Washington, DC and saw the White House and the Capitol. On their way back to Kansas, they stopped off at Six Flags for a day and spent their entire school vacation seeing the country. Said Glen, "When I was in school, I just read about these places. I didn't ever get to see them. My kids get to see these places when we all go out together, and I'd say it has been good for us, not only as a family but also because it has helped them in school as well."

Mary said making the children part of his work has also provided some much-needed reassurance about the part each person plays in the family. "They know dad's out on the road, working so we can have our house and our cars and our vacations together," she said. "Glen does a good job of reassuring them while he's on the road. He calls home at least every other day and they can send e-mails to him—and vice versa—that he can get right there in the cab. I think we're lucky, and we tell him how much we love him and appreciate his hard work every chance we get!"

COMMUNICATION MAKES LIFE EASIER FOR INDEPENDENT COUPLES

Sue and Melvin have led their own lives, even though they've been married for more than 20 years. They met in the military and their relationship survived several assignments that kept them apart for months.

When they retired from the service, Melvin decided to go over-the-road, and Sue decided to continue her career as a purchasing agent and raising their daughter. "That was back before cell phones, so we talked about once or twice a week," Sue recalled. "Because I had to create my own life, Cindy—our daughter—and I often went out to eat and to the movies or shopping at the mall after I got off work. So, whenever Melvin called, his first question was, 'Where were you?'"

As long-distance rates went down and cell phones appeared, Melvin and Sue found they liked talking more often, and they've worked out an agreement about giving each other the "third-degree" long distance. "Now, if one of us is thinking about the other, we just call," Sue said. "It's working better for all of us."

Since their daughter is now living elsewhere with her new career, Melvin and Sue are finding they really enjoy spending more time together, but neither is willing to give up the lives they've led separately all these years. Melvin still loves his over-the-road lifestyle and Sue is now a manager at the company where she's worked for the last 15 years.

"Oh, for vacations, I'll go out with him on the truck, but that's not the life I want," Sue confided. "We've talked about it. I want to be at home, I want my career and my friends, so I doubt I'll ever go out with him full-time."

"I like it that Sue is independent," Melvin admits. "She's always been able to take care of business, which made it easier for me to go out and feel confident that everything would be okay at home. If anything, I probably haven't told her often enough how much I appreciate what she does or what a good job she does. I need to do that."

And Sue makes an admission of her own. "Mel and I have had a great life together - even though we haven't been together much of the time. But I may have taken him for granted more than I should," Sue said. "He's always worked hard. He's never complained and he's always made an excellent living. Ten years ago, he started buying trucks and now has five on the road. He's taken care of all the details, never complained, and has done a fabulous job. I guess we need to take a look at our communication style. Those words of appreciation could go both ways."

If one or both partners plan to make their lives over-the-road together, it is important that both are doing what makes them happy, doing what they love.

Ken grew up in a family where both parents worked and both parents hated their jobs. So when Ken and Barbara met, they talked about the importance of doing what they loved and about being happy with themselves before they could be happy with each other.

Now, 10 years later, they remain unmarried but committed to their relationship. Both drive over-the-road. They've managed to pay off their home and have a place at the lake they both say they don't use as much as they would like, but they're happy and they're doing jobs they love.

"You have to be happy with yourself," Barbara emphasized. "You have to do things that you like, whether it's the work you do on the job or what you do for a hobby, or when you socialize. For example, Kenny and I both like the freedom that comes with driving over-the-road. We talk every day, sometimes twice. When we're home, we like going out. We like live music and we like fishing, so that's what we do."

"One thing that's made our relationship good is that neither of us have been afraid to try something new, and we've given ourselves and each other room to fail," Ken explained. "We take care of ourselves, first, and in doing that, we take care of each other."

The first step to that, they agree, is feeling like you are somebody important. "In my mom's case, she was always somebody's wife, somebody's mother, or somebody's sister," Barbara said. "She never knew that she was somebody, somebody important and talented and beautiful. No matter how her role changes, she's still somebody, but when all of us were grown and out of the house, she went through a real crisis because she wasn't the carpool driver or the room mother any more."

Ken said the next step—after figuring out you're someone important—is to take some time out to actually love yourself. "One time, Barbara and I sat down and wrote what we really liked about ourselves on a piece of paper," he remembered. "We didn't share our lists, but then we wrote down what we liked about each other. It was pretty amazing how close my list was to her list. But you do have to love yourself. It may sound strange to some people, but believe me, until you love and appreciate yourself, you won't be able to love each other."

The couple—whenever they're in town together—often indulge themselves by going to a particularly good restaurant, or spending a little extra to buy good seats at the rodeo or to hear musicians. "Barbara likes dance," Ken said. "It's not something I want to do all the time, but because I know she likes it, we go to dance concerts now and then. And we also go to NASCAR events. And Barbara will be the first to tell you, they're not exactly her thing, but she goes because she knows I like 'em."

In everything they do together—especially dance concerts and NASCAR races—Barbara and Ken are reassuring each other of their feelings. "We do love each other," Barbara affirmed, but we love ourselves, too. We love what we do and we love being together. I'd say we have learned to really have a great life. It isn't always easy, but with a little practice and good communication, you can fulfill your needs and the needs of your partner, too."

REASSURANCE AS A CURE FOR "COUPLE STRESS"

Because everyone is different, when two people come together in a relationship, there's no real way to avoid conflicts. But by developing communication skills and by listening, the relationship can be strengthened so it won't collapse because of long separations or a series of conflicts.

Problems for most begin because people have differences. Those differences can occur in your beliefs, in how you do things, how you view certain circumstances, or in your goals. Here's an example.

Marie has always kept her feelings to herself. She learned to do this by watching her mother endure abuse from her father and then act as though everything was perfect.

Her partner—Joe—is very talkative. You know what Joe thinks about everything because he talks about it. He's verbal, and he comes from a family where every issue was laid out on the table and discussed until a solution was reached.

When Marie met Joe, she was attracted to him because of his talkative style. He was a strong communicator, something Marie wasn't. And Marie was attractive to Joe because she was so quiet and so feminine, as though she had everything under control.

Once they became a couple, Joe started feeling frustrated because he never knew how Marie felt. And, as the days and months passed, these frustrations led to a blow-up.

What the two of them learned after attending counseling is that conflicts arise less often when people feel appreciated, loved, and respected. "We learned to compliment each other every day," Marie said, "and I learned to talk about my feelings more. It took time, but once I found that Joe wanted me to talk about feelings, it became easier and he reassured me every step of the way."

"By resolving this difference in our personal 'styles,'" Joe said, "we also learned that we could resolve other problems by talking about them. And because we try to tell each other we love the other every day—and more often usually—we can sit down and be sane about issues when we have our differences.'

If you think couples get along all the time, you're living in fantasyland. In fact, couples who survive are those who learn how to argue successfully—not aggressively or bitterly but by fighting fairly—and that means no hitting below the belt.

First of all, be positive, not negative. For example, if your spouse doesn't call if he or she is going to be later than you expect, say, "I appreciate it when you call me if you're going to be late."

If you're negative and say, "If you don't tell me what time you're going to finally show up, just expect to eat a burnt dinner."

Listen to the other's feelings without commenting, disagreeing, or going on the defensive. Then discuss the details of the disagreement. It is also important to keep your feelings focused on the issue at hand, not something your partner did six weeks ago.

Finally, negotiate until you agree. In some cases, the final part of the argument may be agreeing to disagree. But remember, negotiation means "give and take." Don't say, "You're the one who is always making a big deal about keeping the house clean, so you clean it." Instead—in negotiating—say, "I heard you say that the house being clean is really important to you. I'll be glad to help on the weekends, just not the minute I walk in the door. Will that help?"

And, once you've had a disagreement, listened, communicated, and then negotiated, remember why you like each other. Make a list of things you enjoy doing together and make time—like a weekly date— to do something on your shared list. Spending special times together and making special memories will allow you to like each other more. And when you love and respect your partner, the next time you argue, it will be a friendlier event.

⚠ AND NOW FOR DESSERT!

The driver swung down from the cab after five hours of hellacious driving through the never-ending construction zones on Interstate 45. Today was his youngest daughter's birthday and he was feeling particularly lonesome.

The truck stop, one of his favorites, would be a good place to get a good meal, refuel, and check in with his dispatcher.

The food. One of the reasons he liked stopping at this "mom and pop" was the food: always good, always fresh. Their specialties were beef stew and homemade chili. That and a big glass of ice tea should pull him out of this funk.

The dining room was as big as a cavern because the truck stop not only served truckers and travelers, but also the people who lived in the small town on the opposite side of the highway. He stood at the door and scanned the room. Sure enough, there were several tables of families, finishing their evening meals.

He thought about his daughter. Six years old today. He had been there when she was born, had cut the umbilical cord as his wife held the squirming and crying newborn. She was, he determined in those first hours of her life, everything he could ever dream of, and his dream continued as she began to crawl, to walk, to talk. and to run into his arms every time he came home from a trip.

The waitress interrupted his remembrance. "Can I seat you, sir," she asked.

"Oh, uh...sure. Just anywhere will be alright."

"Which way you going tonight, north or south?" the woman queried

"Up through Oklahoma, Missouri, and then to Chicago."

"And where's home?"

"Arkansas. My family's there."

She stopped at a table, pulled out a chair, and handed him a menu.

"Today's my daughter's birthday," he said, taking a seat. "Really miss being there."

Another waitress appeared with green pad and pencil in hand.

"Think I'll have beef stew and a glass of tea. Been thinking about how good that tea would taste for the last 100 miles."

The waitress smiled, jotted down his order, and then in a few minutes, returned with the tea. "We're pretty slow right now, so do you mind some company?"

"Heck no," he answered. "Glad to have the conversation."

The waitress told him she was going to the college down the road, studying nursing, and was working here to pay her way through.

The driver pulled out his wallet and showed her a picture of his daughter. It was last year's kindergarten school picture, but there under the plastic was his precious Emma, smiling big enough to reveal her first missing tooth, her delicate blond curls cascading to her shoulders. "Her mama usually puts her hair up in braids or a ponytail. For this picture, she curled it. She's pretty special and today's her sixth birthday."

The two talked about their various roads in life until it was time to serve the driver's dinner.

As the driver sweetened his tea, the cook—a man in his 50s—came out. "Mind if I have a glass of tea with you?" he asked.

"Sure. Come on. Love the company."

As the cook drank his tea and the trucker dug into the heaping bowl of beef stew, the two men shared stories about their families. The cook had two sons. One of them is now in the service and the other is finishing a teaching degree. "We all like to hunt," he said. "Even though we have different talents, we all like to hunt and we spend the holidays on a deer lease every year. Really gives us a chance to catch up."

"My wife's pregnant," the driver volunteered. "I think she would like to have a boy this time, you know, so we would have one of each, but it really doesn't matter to me, one way or another, just as long as its healthy."

He told the cook about his little girl, pulling his wallet out once again to show off her picture. "Her name's Emma. Sure do miss her, especially tonight since its her birthday," he added.

"I've missed a few of those myself," the cook said, "while I was in the service. Hurts like the devil, but a kid's love is unconditional. They never hold it against you. And, in their own ways, they do understand that daddy's got a job to do."

As the cook drank the last of the tea in his glass, he extended his hand. "Have a safe one," he said. "Enjoyed the conversation."

Just as the driver was putting the finishing touches on the delicious stew, the doors to the kitchen opened and the waitresses and kitchen crew paraded out, singing happy birthday and carrying a plate with a frosted sweet roll and a lighted candle in the middle.

"Happy birthday, dear Emma," they sang, and the driver joined in. "We thought since you were missing your family, this would give you a chance to celebrate with Emma tonight," the waitress said.

The trucker stood and hugged each of the singers and then blew out the candle, wishing Emma many, many more happy birthdays.

"Thanks, folks. You don't know how much this means," he said, trying to dodge the lump in his throat.

"We're just glad to do it," the cook said. "Like I told you, most of us have been in your shoes at one time or another. We just wanted to help you make it through this one." "And, just to make this one extra special, we're paying your tab in honor of Emma's birthday."

The trucker shook his head as he walked out into the cool night air. "That's one of the nicest things that's ever happened to me. Kinda restores my faith in my fellow man," he added. And then he looked into the blackness of the night with more stars than he had seen in a long time. "Happy birthday, Emma. And you know, daddy loves you."

Chapter 13

Stress and How to Deal With It

Speed up. Slow down. Change lanes. Four-wheelers cutting me off. There's that burning feeling in my stomach again.

"The weather report says snow on the other side of the mountains. My shoulders and neck ache.

"Snow on the road. Getting further behind in my schedule. I wonder why I didn't sleep last night?

"Traffic slowing down. A wreck ahead. I wonder why I'm exhausted all the time?"

For weeks, Ted noticed aching muscles, loss of appetite, restless sleep, and a complete sense of exhaustion. At first he tried to ignore these problems, but he became so short-tempered and hard to get along with that his family told him to either go to the doctor or get back on the road!

The challenges of truck driving are changing at breakneck speed. More traffic. Tighter schedules. Higher fuel costs. More technology putting pressure on the driver. Time away from family and friends.

So what is going on with Ted? Job stress?

The National Institute for Occupational Safety and Health (NIOSH), which is the federal agency responsible for conducting research and making recommendations for prevention of work-related illness and injury, defines job stress as:

> *. . . the harmful physical and emotional responses that occur when the requirements of a job do not match the capabilities, resources or needs of the worker.*

NIOSH also states that job stress can lead to poor health and even injury.

Job stress is often confused by many with the challenge of a job, but these are two separate and distinct issues. A challenge energizes a driver psychologically and physically. It motivates him or her to learn new skills and master a job. When a challenge is met, a driver feels relaxed and satisfied.

When Ted is challenged with a difficult task, which he accomplishes often, he feels good about his job and about himself. Accomplishing a challenging task is an important ingredient for healthy and productive work. The importance of a challenge in the workplace is probably what people are referring to when they say "a little bit of stress is good for you."

Ted agrees that accomplishing a challenging task is good. He remembers when he was in high school and worked in the summer for his Uncle Joe who had a sign painting company. Needless to say, Ted didn't do much of the sign painting. His job, instead, was mostly hammering and nailing, and nearly all of the hole digging for the signs, which was done by hand.

One hot summer day, when Ted was 15 years old, he and his Uncle Joe drove about five miles west of town where they were going to erect a 12' x 8' sign for a local barbeque restaurant. Ted preferred erecting signs in town. Since the town was located in a river valley, the digging was pretty easy there. Not so west of town. West of town was a high plateau where the soil was very rocky.

After Ted and his Uncle Joe unloaded the digging gear from the truck, Uncle Joe made about two stabs into the dusty rocky ground.

Ted's Uncle Joe glanced up at the hot summer sun and wiped the perspiration from his face with the red bandana he always carried in the rear pocket of his overalls. "Looks like about a two-day job" Uncle Joe said. "Get your lunch and the water jug out of the truck. I got to go back to town to meet a customer. I'll be back to get you about five o'clock."

So Ted dug and perspired, and perspired and dug. And then he dug and perspired some more.

Every so often, a big rig would come by and honk at Ted. As Ted waved and watched the air-conditioned rigs disappear in the distance across the plains, he decided right then and there, on the dusty, rain-starved plains of western Oklahoma, that he was going to graduate from high school and go to truck driving school.

So Ted dug and perspired, and waved and dug, and perspired and waved some more.

Because of the inspiration of the honking air-conditioned rigs and a lot of luck, Ted had finished that two-day job by the time Uncle Joe came back to get him that afternoon. "Great job, boy!" Uncle Joe said as they drive back to town.

That is when Ted declared to his Uncle Joe that he was going to finish high school and become a professional driver so he could drive one of those big air-conditioned rigs.

Because of all the traffic, tighter schedules, higher fuel costs, the aggressive four-wheelers out there, and being gone from his family so much, Ted sometimes thinks driving has gone beyond a difficult task. And he doesn't know if he is having all that much fun anymore.

CAUSES OF JOB STRESS

Nearly all the experts agree that job stress results from the interaction of the worker and the conditions of work. Views differ, however, on the importance of worker characteristics versus working conditions as the primary cause of job stress. These differing viewpoints are important because they suggest different ways to prevent stress at work.

Professionals who study job stress think individual characteristics such as personality and coping style are most important in predicting whether job conditions will result in stress. In other words, what may be stressful for one person may not be a problem for another.

This viewpoint leads to prevention strategies that focus on workers and ways to help them cope with demanding job conditions.

Although the importance of individual differences cannot be ignored, scientific evidence suggests that certain working conditions are stressful to most people. Such evidence leads to thinking that the greatest emphasis should be on changing working conditions rather than teaching the worker how to cope with the existing conditions.

NIOSH's approach to job stress, based on their experience and research, favors the view that working conditions play a primary role in causing job stress. According to NIOSH's view, exposure to stressful working conditions can have a direct influence on workers safety and health.

NIOSH has determined that the following job conditions may lead to stress.

> **The Design of Task.** Heavy workload, infrequent rest breaks, long hours and shift work; and hectic and routine tasks that have little inherent meaning do not utilize a worker's skills and provide little sense of control.
>
> *Drivers have a heavy workload, have infrequent rest breaks, and work long hours. Some drivers feel they have less and less control of the situation because of the heavy traffic and frequent highway construction.*
>
> **Management Styles.** Lack of participation by workers in decision-making, poor communication in the organization, and lack of family-friendly policies.

The typical driver is not involved in many of the decisions regarding their work. "Take this load to Los Angeles and have it there by Friday." Not much sharing of decision-making there. In many situations, once the driver goes on the road, there is very little communication with management. You may have to look far and wide to find family-friendly fleets. While some companies allow drivers to take their significant others, children, and even pets on the road with them, others do not.

Interpersonal Relations.   Poor social environment and lack of support or help from coworkers and supervisors.

Many drivers say the lack of interpersonal relations while on the road is a big problem. No one to talk to. Just drive, eat, sleep, drive, eat, sleep. And then drive, eat, sleep some more. Some companies, as noted above, are addressing the problem of lack of interpersonal relations by letting spouses, children, and pets accompany the driver.

Work Roles.   Conflicting or uncertain job expectations, too much responsibility, too many "hats to wear."

Many drivers said this was not one of their problems. They said the expectations are pretty clear: inspect the rig, load, drive safely, keep accurate records, get along with customers, drive, eat, sleep, and make deliveries on time.

Career Concerns.   Job insecurity and lack of opportunity for growth, advancement, or promotion; rapid changes within the industry for which drivers are unprepared.

Although job insecurity for a professional driver is not often a problem, many drivers feel there is very little opportunity for advancement or promotion in the industry. Maybe they can move on to become a dispatcher, a driver trainer, or a safety director, but compared to the number of drivers on the road, there are not many of those types of jobs. Some drivers purchase a truck or many trucks, but they still drive.

Environmental Conditions. Unpleasant or dangerous physical conditions such as crowding, noise, air pollution, or ergonomic problems.

This is probably the one area that has the greatest negative effect on the professional driver. Factors such as aggressive drivers, poor sleeping conditions, heavy traffic, bad weather, miles and miles of construction, equipment in poor condition, diets high in fat content, lack of physical exercise, and lot lizards disturbing the drivers' sleep are all conditions that lead to stress for the professional driver.

Looking at this list of working conditions, it's clear that being a professional driver can be a very stressful job.

Job Stress and Health

Stress sets off an alarm in the brain, which responds by preparing the body for defensive action, The nervous system is aroused and hormones are released to sharpen the senses, quicken the pulse, deepen respiration, and tense the muscles.

This biological response, which is called the "fright or flight response," is important because it helps us defend against threatening situations. Everyone responds in much the same way in a stressful situation.

This is the response that enabled a truck driver who happened on a wreck on the freeway near a major city in the south to rescue a fellow driver, trapped by a bent steering column and the roof of the crushed cab in his burning rig. The rescuing driver patted out the fire around the trapped driver with his bare hands and straightened the steering column. Then, after squeezing into the cab, he raised the roof of the cab with his back and legs. After removing the injured driver from the wreck, the rescuer got back into his rig and drove off into the night.

The fight or flight response is extremely strong. For the caveman, this response was very useful when he had to fight a saber-toothed tiger for breakfast or defend his family on the frontier.

Today, we don't have to fight many saber-toothed tigers or defend our families on the frontier, but the response is still with us. As we go about our daily lives, we still experience the fight or flight response.

Short-lived or infrequent episodes of stress pose little risk to our health. But when stressful situations go on and on, which happens often in the life of a professional driver, the stress is extremely dangerous. When stressful situations happen often, the body is kept in a constant state of activation with adrenaline pumping, heart beating rapidly, and so forth. This constant state of activity increases the rate of wear and tear on a driver's body.

Ultimately, fatigue or damage results, and the ability for the body to repair and defend itself can become seriously damaged. As a result, the risk of injury or disease increases, and the driver has more accidents or is subject to diseases that could prevent him or her from continuing on the job.

Many studies have looked at the relationship between job and stress, and a variety of ailments. Mood and sleep disturbances, upset stomach, headache, and disturbed relationships with family and friends and coworkers, are examples of the results of stress.

These early signs of job stress are usually easy to recognize. But the effects of job stress on chronic diseases take a long time to develop. Nevertheless, there is strong evidence that job stress plays a major role in several types of chronic diseases such as cardiovascular disease, musculoskeletal disorders, and psychological disorders.

Early warning signs of job stress can include:

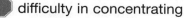 headache

 sleep disturbances

 difficulty in concentrating

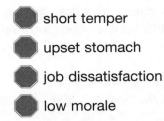

- short temper

- upset stomach

- job dissatisfaction

- low morale

All drivers should watch for these warning signs. They could lead to the following more serious conditions.

- ***Cardiovascular Disease.*** Many studies suggest that psychologically demanding jobs that allow employees little control over the work process increases the risk of cardiovascular disease. Truck driving is a psychologically demanding job. The factors of the job over which the driver has no control, such as aggressive drivers, heavy traffic, highway construction, tight schedules, poor sleeping accommodations, and equipment in poor repair, make the job very psychologically demanding.

- ***Musculoskeletal Disorders.*** On the basis of research by NIOSH and many other organizations, it is widely believed that job stress increases the risk for development of back and upper-extremity musculoskeletal disorders. Driving puts a great deal of stress on the arms, shoulders, and back. If a driver has problems in these areas, they could end a career.

- ***Psychological Disorders.*** Several studies suggest that differences in rates of mental health problems (such as depression and burnout) for various occupations are due partly to differences in job stress levels. While there is no data regarding depression and driving, there are many drivers who openly discuss driver burnout.

- ***Workplace Injury.*** Although more study is needed, there is a growing concern that stressful working conditions interfere with safe work practices and set the stage for injuries at work. The fact that most work-place injuries for truck drivers occur around the truck (getting in and out, loading, and the like) rather than in traffic accidents suggests that stress is a big contributor.

 Cancer, Ulcer, and Impaired Immune Function. Some studies suggest a relationship between stressful working conditions and these health problems. Some medical data suggest a high incidence of ulcers among professional drivers.

Some employers assume that stressful working conditions are a necessary evil, that companies must turn up the pressure on workers and set aside health concerns to remain productive and profitable in today's economy. But research findings challenge this belief. Studies show that stressful working conditions are actually associated with in-creased absenteeism, tardiness, and intentions by workers to quit their jobs, all of which has a negative effect on the bottom line.

Studies of businesses that have policies that benefit workers' health shows that as workers' health increases, the companies' profits increase.

Here are some workplace scenarios which lead to low stress, high productivity, and better health.

Recognition of employees for good work perfor-mance. More fleets are doing a better job of recog-nizing drivers with awards and personal "thank you's" that demonstrate the driver is valued.

Opportunities for career development. Although these are limited in trucking, they are available if you want to learn another facet of the business.

Reducing job stress can be divided into two segments and is illus-trated in the following formula:

Organizational Changes + Stress Management = A Healthy Workplace

"Since I spend 99.99 percent of my time on the road, I don't think organizational changes—such as the ones we

have looked at in this chapter—really have much of an effect on me," Ted said as we discussed this chapter at a local truck stop.

"Sure it's nice when the dispatcher says something nice and brags about the good job I do. Or when someone in the office smiles at me and says 'hello' when I walk though the office on the way to the loading docks. "Sure, I like to get my annual award for safe driving. The banquet is real nice.

The barbeque is really good. My wife looks real nice when she has on her party dress. And my kids smiled and were real proud of me when my name was called for the best driver award. I like hearing the company president brag about the drivers. That was all real nice. But what I really liked about the safe driving award was the bonus that went with it.

"The company wellness program, where I can get a reduced membership at the local health club, doesn't help me that much. If the health clubs were in the truck stops where I spend most of my nights, I would like to exercise a few minutes each day. Sure, I enjoy listening to the company wellness newsletter on tape as I cover my route. Sure, I have learned some good health tips from it. I try to eat less fatty food and walk some most mornings before I start my day.

"Sure, I enjoy using the phone card the company provides the drivers so I can call home daily. My wife can keep me updated about what is going on at home. My children enjoy talking to me and I love hearing about their day. It kind of takes the edge off being on the road all the time. And I don't feel so isolated when I can talk to my family each day.

"It is nice to have that Driver's Counselor back at the headquarters. She has really helped some drivers with their personal problems.

"And sure, I like the company program where my kids can travel with me some in the summer," he continued. "We get

some prime visiting done. They are growing up too fast. It really helps when I can spend some extra time with them.

"And this year, all of my kids are old enough to go to church camp, so my wife can go on the road with me for a few days. I don't know if she is going to be really fired up about spending the night in a parking lot with those lot lizards making their rounds and banging on truck doors.

"You know, before we talked about it, I didn't think the company did much for the drivers. It looks like they are really trying to make life on the road better for us. I must work for a pretty good company."

Chapter 14

Keeping the Faith: Religion on the Road

E ndless miles and countless days away from home base give the professional driver time, time to listen to books and music on tapes, time to commune with Nature and time to think about life's big picture.

Dan Hiser, a professional driver with ABF Freight Systems, Inc., and a member of America's Road Team, has 39 years of experience from over-the-road with national carriers to driving tankers, carhaulers, and flatbeds.

When Dan goes to work everyday, he carries his Bible, along with a collection of inspirational tapes.

"The hardest part about being a professional driver is the lack of closeness with family and friends," he admitted. "And there is loneliness, stress, and isolation. It's not easy, even with e-mail and cellular phones so your family and friends can contact you while you're on the truck. Before, you were gone for long periods of time and could only call home once a week. That was tough.

"But, mainly, being over-the-road meant not being able to roll over and give your husband or wife a hug. Oh, the

communications are there now, but before, a lot of times, there was a lack of trust in relationships. And sharing a religious faith made that trust come easier," he said.

Studies show that those people who have some type of personal faith or an affiliation with a belief-centered group seem to be more successful in dealing with stressful situations, as well as with separations and loneliness.

In Dan Hiser's experience, making a "connection" with his faith while he was out on the road smoothes his path. "Whenever we could, we would stop in at a community church and worship," he said. "Or, if that wasn't available, a lot of truck stops have a Transport for Christ program, usually a truck in their parking lot that offers services several times during the week.

"What I found out is that I do better when I 'connect' with people who have a belief," Hiser continued. "They may not be my personal religious affiliation, but sharing a belief in God made us almost instant friends.

"When I don't have the one-on-one fellowship with people who believe as I do, before too long, I notice that life gets a little more difficult," he said, "and you sometimes have a tendency to get like the rest of the world, and could be anything from cynical and angry to distrusting and frightened of what's coming next. Luckily, with the schedule I have now, I have one time a week to worship and to have fellowship, and it sure helps."

He said listening to American Family Radio has helped him get through some tough days and, whenever possible, he tunes into programming that offers Biblical instruction. "These programs and 'The Bible on Tape' have helped remind me that it is important to stay on my knees whenever I stop driving and what I hear encourages me to keep moving forward. Like I said, it gets me through the day."

"Sometimes when you are on the road, you really have no place to turn but up," said another veteran driver. "And, if you feel out of control, it helps to realize that there is a Higher Power running the show. "My participation in a 12-step pro-

gram many years ago taught me that it is best to step aside, to be aware of the messages you get day in and day out, to actually surrender to this power, and watch as you are guided out of the darkness of your unhappiness."

Jody, a 28-year-old over-the-road professional with more than eight years experience, remembers the feeling of being alone each week she was away from home.

"You have a tendency to slip into what I call pity-parties," she said. "And, if you're not careful, you'll also find yourself totally focused on you and how unfair life is."

She admits, when she first went over-the-road, to overreacting to almost every situation. "If I called my husband—also a driver—and he wasn't exactly where he said he would be, I'd fume for hours. And if I couldn't find him all day, by the end of my shift, my stress level was sky-high and my feelings about my marriage were totally negative. I could imagine everything from Tony being in a terrible accident to being with another woman, all in the same thought. It was torture for me and it wasn't doing our relationship any good either."

One night, after Jody had stopped for her rest, she was having dinner in a truck stop when another woman driver asked to share her table. As their conversation went from business to the events of their day, Jody shared her frustration about not being able to find her husband and her feelings of self-pity.

The other driver, an older and more experienced professional, reached into her backpack and slid a small book across the table to Jody. "Take this book and read it every time you wake up," she counseled. "I'm not promising anything, but I can tell you, it has gotten me through all kinds of problems and it may do the same for you."

The book, titled *One Day at a Time in Al-Anon*, was originally written for family members of alcoholics and offers an inspirational message for every day of the year, covering topics ranging from keeping an open mind and self-esteem to serenity, listening, anger, guilt, gratitude, and frustration.

Jody said that dinner literally changed her attitude, her relationship, and her life.

> *"What we don't stop and think is that we're just human beings and there are many things that are out of our control. Having someplace to turn—whether it is your faith, your belief in God, a tape, or a book—often gives us the strength to continue on down the road," she said.*

Dan Hiser said he usually carries inspirational pamphlets with him on the road and, whenever the opportunity presents itself, he shares these with other drivers, either personally or by leaving the pamphlets on tables in restaurants, on the lavatory in restrooms, or in driver lounges.

> *"When some of the guys I work with are going the same way, we talk about our faith and how our lives are going on another channel on the CB, and it never fails," the veteran driver said. "People will come in on that channel and ask for prayer for something in their lives. So in spite of what some drivers think, the CB radio can be used for good."*

One anonymous CB request for prayer involved a man's young son who was undergoing surgery later that day. And once the drivers guided their trucks onto their different routes, prayers were said, asking for guidance for the surgeons, for strength for the family, and for healing of the youngster.

The group never heard from that particular trucker again, but they agreed that even if talking about the child's upcoming surgery over the CB gave that nameless, faceless driver a few minutes of peace or the feeling of support, it was time well spent.

> *"I try to let drivers know I'm glad to pray for them," said Hiser. "I carry a prayer list at all times because I've found that in a lot of cases, people will come up to another driver and ask for help or prayer when they're not comfortable going up to a pastor.*
>
> *"Bottom line," said Hiser, "we need each other. As professional drivers, we understand the situations that may come*

*up, day in and day out. In some ways, reaching out to fellow
drivers is like being a part of a big support group."*

He tells the story of a driver in his 40s—a driver for a competing
carrier—who Hiser saw regularly in his home town.

*"When we got to know each other and he found out I was a
believer, he started talking to me about his life, about the
losses he had suffered, about mistakes he thought he had
made.*

*"Of course, I had been praying for him to find the guidance
and the path he needed to be happy," Hiser continued.
"About four months ago, he was baptized and that same
driver who was once so confused, so angry, and so lonely,
says he has found a different road. He's at peace where he
was once struggling. And it's not something that happens as
often as I would like, but I'm just glad I was there when he
needed someone to talk to."*

Spiritual Healing

Does a religious belief or a personal faith of any kind answer all of life's
questions or solve all problems?

Spirituality is a mode of inner peace. It provides a way to ease the
pain and suffering of long absences. It can also offer patience and
calm when a driver faces long delays or stressful deadlines.

One of the goals of any group—be it a church, a Jewish congrega-
tion, a meditation group, or an Islamic temple—is to serve those who
come to worship or pray or meditate. Many offer counseling, fellowship, aid, and, most important, an environment of understanding and
encouragement.

These same groups—whether you attend once a week or once
every six months—can provide a safe haven away from all the harsh-
ness the world may offer. Many members admit that they have come
seeking comfort and a sense of belonging without feeling threatened.
And for the most part, these organizations provide a nonthreatening
way to be nurtured and supported.

There is, of course, a reason to be cautious if you are entering a group for the first time and are away from home. Cult expert Rick Ross says, "If a group is too good to be true, they probably are up to something."

Unfortunately, there are groups who prey on the lonely and on people who feel helpless or lost in their lives. So it is important to visit traditional groups of any faith that are well established in a community.

How do you find the best place for meditation, for worship, and for support? Some may prefer a calm meditative and individual environment. Others prefer an upbeat and active format. Decide what best fits your needs and then ask someone you know about where to find this place.

And as a professional driver, your schedule may make it impossible to regularly attend meetings of a particular group. In this case, contact the leader and find out if it would be possible to "connect' with a member or members by telephone periodically. And ask for recommended readings, tapes, or pamphlets to help you increase your understanding.

Some groups offer daily meditation or prayers on telephone prayer lines. Others offer 800 numbers, inviting anyone—members and non-members, alike—to call in requests and needs. Still other groups offer monthly meditation. The Methodist Church has, for years, published collections of daily inspiration consisting of a prayer, Bible verses, and stories of others in "The Upper Room." Unity Church publishes "The Daily Word," another small pocket-sized book with two- to three-minute daily readings.

Religion and the Internet

With the advent of the Internet, those who travel professionally can now "attend" worship services and "connect" with others of the same belief over the World Wide Web. The following are a few suggested sites, although you will find any number of options by surfing the Net.

Christianity   http://www.fontbonne.edu/libserv/fgic/fgic.htm or www.crossroads.com

Judaism: http://www.mavensearch.com

Buddhism: http://www.buddhanet.net

Hinduism: http://www.hindunet.org

For more religious listings, visit www.beliefnet.com.

The Internet is also a good place to for study and learn more about your faith. You can download and search many religious topics. One Web site that offers a complete study of every chapter of the Bible is www.ccel.org. And some Internet sites are specifically designed for over-the-road professional drivers. Visit www.truckersforchrist.org. Because this particular group not only understands the demands of the trucking industry but also is dedicated to reaching out to drivers, this site is able to provide services specifically designed for truck drivers. They have the Bible on tape and offer a free packet of material when you contact them.

Others to try are http://www.christiantruckers.homestead.com/ or www.transportforchrist.org. These Web sites offer online services, as well as listings of chapels and church services on the road or at truck stops.

If you have a prayer request, many of these sites have prayer groups that can pray with you or for you. And if you've never thought about it in this way, prayer or meditation is an excellent way to talk through your problems and feelings. As one driver said recently, "When I have a chance to pray, I actually can get things off my chest. In fact, sometimes my prayers are used for 'venting' more than praying."

For Your Family

Having a place to go when seeking reassurance, encouragement, and support is also important for your family or those you care about. When you're out on the road for days or weeks at a time, those you love experience the same loneliness, frustration, and anxieties you may find yourself feeling.

Finding a group for this nurturing and peace of mind will offer your family strength to make it through the days you are not there. Friendly, caring groups in churches, the Salvation Army, synagogues, temples, meditation groups, and support groups of all kinds may also be a resource to offer assistance while you are away.

Some larger carriers often provide support groups for the stay-at-home partners of their drivers. In addition to providing a better understanding of the demands of life on the road, these groups also provide a second set of ears when others don't seem to be listening.

And once again, fellowship is important. Children may find opportunities on sports teams, in school groups, or in church, synagogue, or temple youth programs. Established programs of faith may also offer opportunities for family members to grow, surrogate grandparents, and other support for your family while you are on the road.

Any job is easier when you have help. A personal faith often provides that help we all need—in one way or another, at one time, or every day of the week—so we don't have to feel like we're out there doing it all by ourselves.

Back in the days before the CB radio when truck stops offered bunk houses behind the fuel stop instead of motel rooms, drivers often slept in the same room with 20 or 30 other drivers. Dan Hiser said in those days, you could leave your keys in your truck and no one would drive it off.

"Back then, there was a strong bond between drivers, so you never went too long, feeling like you were alone out on that highway.

"Back in the bunkhouse days, we'd often trade stories and eventually get to where we knew each other pretty well," Hiser recalled. "We supported each other, face-to-face, and we knew we were part of a proud tradition.

"It often wasn't put into words, but we knew we were the lifeblood of our country, and we all saw the highways as arteries, all leading to the heart of the nation. And whatever our race or faith, we all shared the same feeling, the same sense of pride and accomplishment every time we'd complete a run. Of course, times have changed, but as drivers, we need to remind ourselves that we're all part of a bigger picture.

"In many ways, driving is character building," Hiser concluded.

"Back when I was younger, most guys and girls grew up by going into the service. Today the same thing is happening on the road. We're all out here making a living, but we're doing a lot of growing, too, and having a faith makes the whole process just a lot easier."

NEVER FORGET TO PASS IT ON

His truck had stopped cold. He tried the ignition. No luck. He tried again.

Just out of Truckee, California, on a Sunday night.

He fumbled for his cell phone in the dark, feeling the cold already clamping its icy fingers around the cab. He prayed the phone's battery was strong enough for a couple of calls.

He called Truckee information and asked the operator for road service, envisioning himself having to trudge through the freezing night for help. A number was given and he dialed. The man at the other end—Butch—said it would take about 30 minutes to get there, but he would be there, guaranteed.

The driver reached into the sleeper and pulled a blanket to fold around him. His teeth were beginning to chatter, but he knew Butch whatever-his-name-was would be on his way shortly.

Within 30 minutes, the tow truck's headlights stabbed through the darkness. Very little other traffic had passed during the entire ordeal.

The tow truck's door opened and a man on crutches eased himself out. Together, the men decided the truck's battery needed a charge and worked to get it started. With a few tries, it was purring as usual.

"How much do I owe you for your help?" the trucker asked.

Butch smiled. "Bet you could use a hot cup of coffee, couldn't you? I've got a thermos in my truck."

As the two sipped the chill-chasing liquid in the tow truck's cab, the trucker asked again. "How much do I owe you?"

Butch looked away for a moment. "No charge."

The trucker tried to argue.

"No. Years ago during Desert Storm, somebody helped me out without asking for pay," Butch explained. "I lost my legs but I got home to my family. And the guy who pulled me out just told me to find someone else who needed help and to pass it along. That's what I'm doing."

The two parted that night. Butch heading back to Truckee and the trucker went on his way to Reno. But after that incident, the trucker was a different man.

About 10 years later, the trucker was driving his route when he saw an SUV pulled over on the shoulder of the road. The left rear tire was obviously flat and the driver was having a problem.

He pulled his rig behind the four-wheeler and jumped down to see what he could do. The young man—on his way to college for the fall semester—had a brand new SUV and didn't know how to change the tire. "I feel so stupid," the youngster confessed, "but I've never had to change a tire before."

"No problem," the trucker reassured. "I've changed more than my share. It'll only take a minute."

When he was through changing the tire, the trucker took off his gloves and was about to say good-bye and get back on the road.

"But I want to pay you for your trouble," the college-bound teen said.

"Nope. Not necessary," the trucker replied and quickly told him the story about losing power in the pass near Truckee that year long ago. "Don't get to help people very often, but this is my way of passing along a good deed that veteran did for me. And I'll just ask you, not for payment, but whenever you have a chance to help someone, just pass along the good turn."

The SUV driver was reluctant but finally accepted the trucker's offer. And as he drove into the night, like the trucker 10 years before, the SUV driver left the scene a different person, ready to do a good deed and to pass on the help he had received from the trucker traveling the same road.

Chapter 15

Staying Close to Your Most Important People

When Frank goes on the road, he says goodbye to his three children and then goes out to do his pretrip and start his truck. When his wife hears the engine rev, she goes out and they have their private goodbye. "We've been doing it this way for so long, it's almost a reflex," said Margaret, Frank's wife of 15 years.

She admits that this is one of the most difficult parts of Frank's job, but said she's been lucky to have support of family, friends, and her church when he's away.

Mona and Jim are not married but have been together for eight years. Their goodbyes are really not "goodbyes," she said. "We've made it a point to never say 'goodbye' when Jim leaves for the road. We just say, 'See you next week' or "See you in two weeks.' 'Goodbye' just sounds too final.

And Julie and Scott have also developed a ritual since Scott started driving two years ago. "We say goodbye the night before and then he leaves before I wake up," said Julie, who's expecting in about three months. "It's hard. Sometimes I cry because I know how the 'missing' feels, but we usually make it just fine. We talk several times a day, now that cell phone minutes are more affordable, and some of the wives at the company where Scott works say they're so accustomed to their husbands being gone, they probably wouldn't know what to do if their spouses took 8-to-5 jobs."

Most professional drivers are on the road a great deal. For new drivers, this means their families are constantly making adjustments. Most over-the-road drivers and their families say the hardest part is dealing with long periods of separation.

Said one spouse whose wife is on the road two weeks out of every month, "Sometimes it feels like this is a single-parent family. I know she's just a phone call or an e-mail away, but when she's on the road— and believe me, she makes twice the money I do—every decision falls on my plate. We have family close by, so there are plenty of hands and plenty of substitute moms to help when they're needed. But I won't lie to you, it is a struggle when Brenda's gone, but we continue to find ways to make mom's absence easier for everyone."

It is certainly not rocket science, but it is definitely worth repeating: You can't expect to go to work, be gone a week or two, then come home and expect everyone to jump around to take care of you.

Unless you need some quiet time when you first come in from the road, you need to be aware that your partner, your family, and your loved ones need lots of attention and care from you as well.

Here's one example. Riley and Donna are raising a granddaughter. She's been with them for four years and is almost five. While Riley's on the road, Donna is there as a mom and a dad for her. But when Riley is between trips, his granddaughter demands his time, especially if she's not feeling well. Only Riley can hold her. Only Riley can kiss it to make it feel better when she scrapes a knee or bumps an elbow.

Wayne, a driver for the past 20 years, and his family have been to counseling to help everyone cope with his absences and his return home. "It's not hard to see. When you are away, your partner takes over everything from paying the bills to dealing with a busted washing machine," Wayne said. "When I was on the road, she might tell me something was broken, but I certainly wasn't much help when it came time to actually do something about it.

"Then, when I came home, instead of her needing help with stuff, she'd tell me she had taken care of it. That made me feel bad, to tell you the truth. Before we went to counseling, it really made me feel like less of a man."

Wayne and Billie did go to counseling, along with their two teenaged sons. "My boys told the counselor that while I was gone, they followed one set of rules. And when I came home, I laid down another set. That confused everybody and before I went out again, most of us were pretty angry."

Through counseling, Wayne's family learned to communicate more. Wayne learned to maintain the rules Billie had set for the boys when he returned home. Billie learned how Wayne felt and could do more to make him feel okay about their situation. And their sons learned that while dad was on the road making money to support the family, their part was to keep things on an even keel at home. Said 15-year-old Tim, "I used to resent dad being away so much, missing my games and just not being here. The counselor helped me understand that dad's being on the road was the reason I get to go to a good school, live in a nice house, and have all I have. I wasn't respectful enough when he came home. I guess I felt he was intruding. Now I know it's not that way."

For any relationship and for any family where there's an over-the-road driver, help is often necessary for everyone cope with the long absences. And those drivers who have been through it and learned to reassure their families said the effort pays big returns.

So where do you begin?

1. First, there are many ways to help your family accommodate your absences like developing strong social ties in the community with friends, organizations, and church, synagogue, or temple.

2. Next, take a little time to prepare everyone for your departure. Show your partner and/or your children where you'll be traveling on a map. Make plans to e-mail each other or to make regular contact with phone calls.

3. Communicate often while you are on the road.

4. Make sure that your time at home is quality time spent with your family.

Maintaining Friends and Family

When Janet first went on the road, she felt as though she were giving up her circle of friends. "Well, we used to get together once or twice a week, and we talked on the phone every day or met after work or whatever," she said. "If I was going to be out of town for two or three weeks at a time, I would be left out. We would have nothing in common. I would be an outsider."

Whether or not Janet maintains her friendships with the group is really up to Janet. Just because she's working out of town, she can still keep in touch with phone calls (not that expensive with a phone card), or through e-mails from her truck if she's got the equipment or from plug-ins at truck stops, Internet kiosks, or at most public libraries wherever she stops en route.

For drivers with families, it is important to have a circle of friends and family that will be there to support your family while you're out of town. This is for your peace of mind as well as your family's. Don and Debra were close to their neighbors before Don went to work as a professional driver. When he found he would be away for two or three weeks at a time, he knew he could count on their friends in the neighborhood to help out whenever Debra needed someone.

"If your wife's car breaks down, who can she call?" Don asked. "It is important for you to know the answer to that question, and it's important for your partner or your spouse to know who you would call for help if you were there."

If your son needs a role model and you aren't there to provide day-to-day guidance, who would you choose to guide him? Usually, there's someone in your extended family, someone in the neighborhood, or someone at church you would entrust with this important task. And if there's not anyone close by, most communities have a group like Big Brother/Big Sister that can spend time with growing children in the absence of mom or dad.

We have all heard the phrase, "It takes a village to raise a child." And for the most part this is true. To help ease the burdens of parenting, you need friends, family, and child care providers that can help raise your children and take care of them when you are gone. Don't just depend on one person, and don't expect your husband or wife at home to spend every moment with the kids. Remember, they need timeouts, time away from the kids, whether it's a chance to run to the grocery store by themselves or a morning getting a haircut and a manicure without the little darlings asking questions or making demands.

So you are about to leave and it's time to say good-bye. How do you handle it with your family so it's not so hard on them?

First, always be open and honest. Most very young children have no concept of time. They don't understand that "tomorrow" actually means the next day until they are older. But be frank with them. Tell them you'll be gone for a week. Tell them you'll call every night. Tell them you'll send e-mails from the road. But never try to sneak away, especially from the children. They need to know that you are leaving and they need to be reassured that you are coming back in one week or two.

Some children may need to be told the day before if they are extremely anxious. Other people need a week, if possible, to prepare. And all the time you're there with them, keep reassuring them that mom or dad will miss them, but that you're going to be okay and they're going to be okay, and when you get home, you'll get to spend more time together.

Let everyone know when you are leaving and when you are coming back. A calendar works well as a visual that the entire family can see. It also gives them an idea of when to expect you back to begin the readjustment period. In some families, the children have a ritual of circling the day mom or dad will be back and then marking off each day—like a countdown—to mom or dad's return.

If you travel a lot, be concerned about others' feelings and tell them yours. It is important for people to talk about what they think instead of bottling up those feelings inside. Your spouse may work out the children's difficulties with your leaving, but you're the one who should be talking about why you leave, what you want to do when you return, and how you can keep in touch while you're on the road.

When you're talking with a child about going out on a trip, give them plenty of room to share their feelings about your absence. It may be something like, "There's a father-daughter banquet, and I'll have to take grandpa and that's not what I want to do." Or, it could be, "Dad, when you're gone, mom and I get along fine and then when you come home, we always get into arguments and I don't like that."

Taking time to talk and share feelings may not always be the nicest conversations, but at least each one has an opportunity to be honest and up-front with what they go through during long absences.

Tommy had grown up with his father as an over-the-road driver. As he got into the awkward years of his early teens, he saw his father's coming back home as an intrusion. When this came out during counseling after months and months of conflict, Tommy, himself, was surprised at his true feelings. "I didn't know I saw dad as an intruder," he admitted. "All I knew was that when dad got home, I felt pushed to the side."

Today, Tommy and his dad make "dates" to spend time together for hunting, fishing, building a home project, or whatever time allows. Tommy and his dad also make a big effort to communicate more and to be honest about their feelings. "During counseling, my dad said he felt left out, and may have been coming on too strong when he came home and felt like he needed to take over," Tommy said. "Knowing how he felt, I could see how he would come home and everything would be going like clockwork and he felt unneeded, although we all needed him, still need him."

Most companies work very hard to get over-the-road drivers home for important family events like births, graduations, marriages, and the like. However, events like birthday parties, school programs, or band concerts may be missed by those who drive heavy schedules.

If you're going to be out of town, and will miss a special event in your partner's life or in the life of a child, try to acknowledge these special times in special ways from the road. But don't overpromise and then underdeliver. This means if you can't make it back in time, don't tell people you will be there.

Most people—and especially children—would rather be surprised that you came instead of feeling disappointed because you said you were coming and then didn't get home in time.

Communicating from the Road

When you are away, communications can be difficult. Your partner, your spouse, your kids, or family and friends may miss you terribly while you're away, so when you are home, make sure to take time to comfort them.

How do you do this? By reassuring them that you like what you do, that you have a good job, and it means you have to be away some of the time. Tell them about what you do, day in and day out. If your company's rider policy permits, take family members with you on the road from time to time. Let them see you at work. Let them see you have time to miss them as much as they miss you.

In addition, stay in touch while you're on the road. This doesn't mean a phone call every so often to remind people who you are. Really try to make an effort to stay involved while you are away. Here are some suggestions in addition to periodic phone calls from the road to let people know you're thinking about them.

- Send thoughtful cards, small gifts, and notes to your family.

- Send e-mails and e-greeting cards. Try http://www.bluemountain.com. They're free.

- Have someone mail your child's artwork or good papers for you to see. Compliment them on a job well done.

- Send home things you find along the way with a note saying that you are thinking about them. It doesn't have to be a big deal. One driver sends things he finds when he stops his rig—like a bird feather or a smooth pebble or a funny bumper sticker—all of which mean so much more when they come from you.

Write letters, especially to children. They don't have to be pages and pages. Just a half-page, encouraging them to write back, and to let them know you love them and are thinking about them will mean so much.

Postcards of places away from home also work well. And if the children save all your destination postcards, they will have something other kids don't have for their geography lessons or for show-and-tell. Make certain these cards show interesting places. You may want to scope places out and send postcards, talking about this place as a possible vacation spot for the family next summer.

Nowadays, one of the cheapest ways to keep in touch is by e-mail. One truck stop in Bordentown, NJ, has a computer room where you can either plug in your laptop or buy a time card for $5 to spend sending e-mails. If you have equipment in your truck or frequent truck stops with plug-ins, a laptop would be a good investment. This allows you to "talk" through e-mails to your family while you are gone. Some Internet providers have chat rooms so you can talk to the folks at home in real time.

When you do call from the road, what do you talk about?

One of the easiest things to talk to your family about is memories you share such as the fishing trip the last time you were home or the good papers your kids brought from school last week. Remind them of the good times you spent together. Tell them that you can't wait to be with them again. Reassure them of your love and tell them that you miss them. Don't forget to let them talk, too, to tell you all of the important things that are happening in their lives.

Families with parents who don't travel often have a "what happened in third grade" as a dinner topic several times a week, so their school-aged children are encouraged to share what's going on in their lives. Drivers can do the same thing through phone calls or e-mail messages from the road.

Each person you speak to from the road—whether an elderly parent, spouse or partner, or child—all have things they are interested in. It might be your father's garden or your child's new friend at school. It might be your wife's Bible study group or her yoga class.

When you're on the road, remember that they have lives while you're not there, and the trick is to be able to plug into those lives. That way, when you do talk, you have something to talk to them about besides just the things you've seen or experienced. Phone calls and e-mails can't all be about you. Your family needs your questions about what they're doing to feel important. And your acknowledgement of accomplishments lets them know you really care, even if you're hundreds of miles away.

It is also important when you communicate from the road to make sure you let your significant other know that you appreciate what he or she does when you are away. You know your job is hard, but did you ever think of those living at home? Thank them for taking care of the house, the children, the pets, and the finances.

Jill, a trucker's wife, said that the reason she left her husband was because he never told her what a good job she was doing. "I kept waiting but all he wanted to talk about was how hard his job was, how rough customers were, or how awful waitresses are to truck drivers," she recalled. "Never once, never once did he ask me how I was doing, how I felt. It was always all about him. Finally, I saw myself disappearing, so I went to counseling. He wouldn't come with me."

The Readjustment Period

When you go over-the-road, your family has to adjust to you being gone. And when you return, they have to go through another adjustment. And so do you, although you may not realize it.

Whatever the situation, don't expect your family to drop everything and be ready for you, especially if you come home unexpectedly. You might think this is a wonderful surprise. After all, your family has been begging you to come home. But it may not be such a good time, especially if your children have something planned and then have to miss it because dad came home unannounced, and they felt they should stay home rather than go on with their plans. This type of situation could easily cause resentment or even worse, a fight.

Like it or not, if your family is going to survive, they have to have their own lives while you are away. They may have their own schedules and plans. And when you come in from the road, you'll often see a need to work around their plans.

Your significant other may play cards with friends every Thursday night. Allow him or her to continue with the activities that are normally on the schedule. And your children may have a birthday party or a soccer game on the calendar, so let them go. For sporting events, if there's a chance for you to go, be sure to make every effort to be there to cheer them on. As you know already, your presence means a lot.

It is a good idea to keep two family calendars, especially with growing children. Keep one in the truck and one on the wall at home. Make sure everyone's schedule is written down. When you call home from the road, update your truck calendar so you'll know what everyone is doing, from Brownie Scout meetings to baseball games and from poker night to the church Christmas program. By keeping two calendars, you'll know what everyone is doing and can ask them about these events from the road. This schedule also allows for no surprises. With an up-to-date calendar, the whole family knows what is going on.

If, when you arrive back at home base, your family has plans that don't include you, why not take some personal time? After all, you probably deserve it. What do you enjoy? You can read a magazine, go play pool, work in your woodshop, or watch a movie. This is a perfect time for you to get some well deserved rest and relaxation.

When You Are Home

If you want to be a success, your job doesn't stop when you park your rig. Relationships and parenting were designed to be a two-person job. Always take time to let those at home know that you appreciate them.

Janice wasn't shy about complaining when husband Ted came off the road. "When he sets foot in this house, he immediately starts complaining about the traffic or a grumpy customer or a smart-alecky dispatcher," she said. Janice had grown tired of trying to be supportive when Ted came home. She was weary of hearing his problems when she had problems, too.

Their counselor recommended that Ted leave his problems in the truck and to walk into their home with a smile.

"It felt like he was angry at us," Janice later explained. "He was in a foul mood and we were so looking forward to him coming home.

Now, Ted walks in and gives everyone a hug. Then, he asks them about their day and what he missed when he was away. He and Janice have an agreement: they will take time to talk about Ted's problems and they definitely talk about his trip, but they save the negative topics until he's been home awhile.

Ted also makes an effort to spend a little alone time with each family member.

This one-on-one is especially important for children of all ages. For little ones, it may be holding them in your lap and reading a favorite story, or building something out of blocks or coloring in a coloring book.

For older kids, you may only have to be in the same room watching them color a picture or sharing a favorite TV program. The main thing is that you are there. It's that you are available to help. And, no, you don't have to finish everything on your honey-do list, but be prepared to make up for lost time by hand-holding, hugging, sharing a sunset, or a walk around the block.

If you have children, you might want to contact the child's teacher or activity leader. Explain that your job takes you out of town for a week or two at a time, but if you're interested, offer to volunteer when you are at home. Most teachers, scout leaders, coaches, and Sunday School leaders will appreciate your time, however little and however periodic. And your children will be proud to have you take part in their lives.

Developing Family Traditions

Even if your job takes you away from home several times a month, some drivers have found that developing those special traditions with your partner, your spouse, and/or your family are more meaningful than anyone thought.

When you develop traditions, you are giving yourself and those close to you something to plan on, something to look forward to, and something to prepare for.

Ways that you can build traditions may include:

- dinner together
- reading bedtime stories
- devotionals
- game or movie night
- driving around the community to see holiday lights
- putting together a model airplane or race car each time you're home
- storytelling night
- scavenger hunts around the neighborhood
- visiting a park
- having a picnic, even if it's the dead of winter and the picnic has to take place on the living room floor

The main point of these traditions is to have routines. The human body was designed to work on a schedule. People begin to have problems when they don't know what to expect and cannot depend on anything. Just like you have a schedule, your family needs a schedule, too.

Professional over-the-road driving isn't always easy on the family, so it is important for you to be sensitive to your spouse, partner, parents, children, and their needs. If you work hard to make the adjustments easy, you are sure to be a success.

50 WAYS TO KEEP HIS OR HER MOTOR RUNNING AND YOUR RELATIONSHIP HITTING ON ALL PISTONS

You've just made a 2,000 mile turnaround. You're in need of a good hot shower, sleeping in your own bed, and some down-to-earth attention from your favorite person. Here are a few suggestions to help fan the flames of your relationship.

1. Surprise your favorite with eleven red roses and one white rose. Attach a note that reads: "In every bunch there's one who stands out - you're it!"

2. Fake a power outage at home. Without TV to distract, a computer to work on, no heat, no stove, no light, you'll have no choice but to get out the candles, cuddle around the fireplace, and slip into one hot, romantic mood!

3. The next time you leave on a long trip, surprise your partner with a bracelet or wristwatch inscribed with "I always have time for you."

4. Attach a $100 bill to a favorite lingerie catalog with a note saying, "You choose!"

5. Celebrate that one big event where the two of you got together every year. Make it a celebration (that means more than a card).

6. Spend a week practicing "Even-Day/Odd-Day" at your house: On even days, it's your turn to be romantic, and on odd days it's your partner's turn. See who can be the most creative

7. Following a wonderful massage or bubble bath, wrap him or her in a towel that you've warmed in the dryer.

8. Trophy shops are great places to find ideas to make your partner feel special. Just think of the romantic possibilities of plaques, medals, ribbons, nameplates, certificates, and banners. And they all can be personalized, engraved, lettered. or monogrammed.

Outrageous

Want to do something really different? Here are some thought-starters to make life more romantic when you're home from the road.

1. After a wonderful dinner, drop in on a favorite karaoke bar and surprise your partner by getting up and singing "your song" to him or her.

2. Kidnap him or her! Drive in circles and then arrive at a romantic inn or other weekend destination. If you have kids, get grandma to baby-sit and spend one night. Make sure there's a Jacuzzi.

3. Make a GIANT greeting card out of a refrigerator carton and put it on the lawn to greet your honey when he or she arrives home.

4. Does your partner love M&Ms or gumballs or gum-drops? Fill a one-gallon glass jar with them as a gift.

5. For special effects during a candlelight supper, buy a little hunk of dry ice from a local ice house, put it in a bowl of water, and place it on your serving tray. You'll create amazing white clouds of environ-mental friendly smoke!

6. Try this one for effect. Slow-dance at a restaurant when there's no music playing. But call ahead to make sure you're not causing any problems with the restaurant's liquor license, which may not allow dancing within a certain distance of the bar.

7. Everybody thinks it is romantic to eat dinner by candlelight, so here's a new twist. Eat breakfast by candlelight.

8. Take your "favorite" on a surprise two-week vacation.

9. Many couples have "His" and "Hers" matching towels, but here are some other ideas: "His" and "Hers" matching silk pajamas, motorcycles, T-shirts, overnight bags (have them packed at all times), jack-o-lanterns at Halloween, rocking chairs, heart-shaped tattoos, Christmas tree orna-ments, tennis rackets, beach towels.

Affordable

If you're light on cash but heavy into love, try these affordable ideas.

1. Spend the entire day in bed watching romantic movies.

2. Want to spend the evening making wishes on falling stars? The earth passes through the Perseides Meteor Belt around August 12th every year, which usually results in spectacular shooting star shows for two to three nights.

3. This one may sound cheesy, but try it anyway. Buy a lottery ticket. Give it to your partner with a little note attached: "I hit the jackpot when I met you!"

4. Want him or her to remember how you feel? Sit down with a tape recorder and just talk to your partner for ten minutes. Then gift-wrap it and mail it.

5. Call a local radio station and request a special love song to be dedicated to your partner. Make sure he or she is listening!

6. Mail your partner a Rolodex card with your name and number on it. Write on it: "Your instant resource for love. Call when lonely."

Fast but for Sure

If you don't have as much time as you'd like for love, try these swift and sweet romantic ideas:

1. Write "I love you" on the bathroom mirror with a piece of soap or lipstick.

2. Have "your song" playing when your partner returns home. If you don't have a "song," try "Theme from Ice Castles" or "Theme from Love Story."

3. When out together in public, make wicked eye contact across the room and wink at your partner. He or she will get the message.

4. On your partner's birthday, send a "thank you" card to his or her mother and father.

5. Make this a tradition. Every time you share a glass of wine, whisper a toast to one another

6. Splurge and buy a whole "family of products" in the fragrance of his or her favorite perfume (bath powder, soaps, cremes, candles, and the like). Then offer a candlelight massage.

Classic

These may be corny, but they are tried and proven techniques.

1. Spread rose petals all over the bedroom. Sometimes, more enterprising lovers will leave a trail of petals from the front door to the bedroom or shower.

2. Want to go back to Victorian times? Make a gift of a fine gold locket with your photo or a lock of your hair inside (or maybe a photo of the two of you).

3. Bring home one small, unexpected gift every time you come in from the road.

4. Before you leave for a long road trip, give your partner a bouquet of one flower for each day that you'll be away. Attach a note that says something like this: "These symbolize the love, joy, and laughter we'll share together when I get home."

5. Spend one hour hugging, holding hands, and talking when you arrive back home.

Chapter 16

Managing Your Money

In the United States today, more than 40 percent of all families spend more than they earn. The average household has 13 or more credit or payment cards. One credit counseling agency reports 96 percent of Americans never achieve financial independence, and on the average, Americans carry about $5,800 in credit card debt annually.

Add to this the fact that many credit card holders only make the minimum monthly payment on that debt. And by current calculations, on a debt of $5,800, it would take about 30 years to pay off.

What's wrong with this picture?

Let's get to know Tara and her family. Tara has been driving a truck for nine years. She works hard. So does her husband, who drives for the same firm. Together, they make a pretty good salary. They have two kids, one six and one eight.

Last year, Tara decided she wanted to change her "financial lifestyle." She was tired of working hard and paying out almost every last penny, so she and her husband went to a credit counseling agency.

"They told us to cut up all but one credit card and to keep that only for emergency use," Tara said. "That one act—and it was painful to cut up those cards—has stopped us from overspending."

The credit counselor also pointed out ways credit card companies go after your hard-earned dollars. "They told us not to take up a credit card company's offer when they came in the mail," she said. "They also told us that if we did get a new card, to watch their annual fees and their nonuse fees, and to watch the monthly statements to make sure they didn't raise our interest rates."

The counselor also told Tara and her husband to make out a monthly budget, something neither one was too excited about doing. "But we decided if we wanted to get out of the hole we'd dug for ourselves, we needed to get serious about our finances," Tara recalled.

A budget simply tells you where your money goes. In trucking terms, it is a map of your daily expenses. You would not just jump in the truck and go. It is important to have a plan of where you are going and what you are doing.

So let's follow the signs toward more financial stability.

Creating a Budget

To create a budget, the first step is to log your daily expenses. Get a notebook or receipt book and keep track of every dime you spend, from the $3.00 for a trade magazine to the $5.00 for a cup a coffee. This may be a surprise in itself, and it may also provide some insight into where your money is going.

Here is an example of a daily log.

Pymt. Type	Date	Payee	Amount	Category
Ck. #1584	2/22/01	Office Max	12.91	Office expense
Cash	2/24/01	Dr. Smith	10.00	Medical expense
ATM	2/27/01	Burger Barn	5.36	Dining expense
ATM	2/28/01	Randall's	70.41	Groceries
Ck. #1585	2/28/01	Watch World	39.02	Misc.

Also look at the advances you may be drawing through Comchek or T-chek to cover necessities. You may be surprised at how much you're drawing to send home.

Next, get all of your bills for a month including utilities, phone bills, credit card bills and rent or mortgage payments. This, with your daily log, is your personal cash flow. Subtract this from your monthly income and you will get an idea of the money that is going in and out.

Hopefully, it will be a positive number. If not, you need to really start adjusting your spending before you get deeper and deeper into debt.

One helpful way to keep track of your income and expenses is to use a computer program like Microsoft Money or Quicken. Not only will it help keep track of daily spending, but it also helps you get a handle on your monthly bills.

So let's review.

1. Record your daily expenses

2. Add your monthly bills

3. Subtract your expense from your income

Now you're ready to move to the next step. Did you find any surprises? Where is your money going? Are there ways to cut expenses?

When you keep track of your spending, it is much easier to manage your money. Instead of blindly using that credit card or writing a check, you will know exactly where the money is going and if you have money available for any extra purchases.

Saving Money

There are not many things you can do with fixed expenses like your mortgage and utilities, but you may be able to adjust your variable expenses, those entertainment costs like restaurant dining or purchasing magazines.

Whenever you are on the road, you are even more inclined to spend cash on food and entertainment. Yes, those videogames don't cost much per game, but some people can't get up after only one game. And some even spend an hour or so playing.

So it is important to keep track of your spending. Set limits and stick to your budget. Otherwise you could cut into your trip profits.

Paycheck – Expenses = Profit

A good way to start saving is by trying to save $3.00 a day. That's a beer or a diner breakfast. After a month, you will have almost $100. If you continue saving for a year, you will have over $1,000. It's that simple.

You can save money on the road by planning ahead. When you are going to take a trip, buy your groceries ahead of time. Not only will you save tons of money but you will also eat healthier.

For entertainment, check out your local library. They have books, books on tape, movies, and CDs that you can borrow for three weeks at a time. Some also have online renewals so if your trip is longer, you can recheck books on the Internet.

Another way to save on entertainment is to subscribe to magazines at home instead of purchasing them at the truck stop. You could save up to 50% off the newsstand price.

For some professional drivers, long-distance calls can eat into profits each month. Take time to search for a plan that suits your needs and call during nonpeak hours. Also, be aware of hidden surcharges and fees. Make sure you get the best deal. Your company may offer some lower cost phone cards or you might want to try prepaid phone cards with a low cost per minute rate. This way, you won't end up with a shock at the end of the month when you get your cellular bill.

Credit and Debit Cards: Friend or Foe?

Now let's take a look at credit and debit cards.

First of all, you should not use credit cards for money that you don't have. This practice could get you into trouble. We will discuss how to get out of debt later in this chapter. When using a credit card, you should plan to pay off the entire balance at the end of each month, and pay them off on time to avoid finance charges and late fees. A $100 debt could turn into a $500 one very quickly with finance charges and late fees. So know your interest rates and penalties.

A good way to stay out of trouble is to record your credit card charges in your check register or daily log. This is good record-keeping practice. And it will also keep you on track and eliminate surprises.

Avoid ATM machines that have bank charges. Find a bank that does not charge a fee to use it and get cash only from these machines. This may mean you get cash at home and not on the road. It is still important to remember to keep track of the cash you spend because it will disappear quickly on small items if you don't plan.

You should never get an advance on your credit card. The charges for advances are outrageous and will stop you dead in your tracks.

Managing Your Debt

The Consumer Credit Counseling Service points to the following as a list of danger signals for family finances.

1. You miss monthly payments on charge cards or only make minimum payments.

2. You can't save money, or if you do save, you find yourself dipping into savings to pay credit card payments.

3. You have a consolidation loan—to pay off credit card debt—and you're paying enormous interest on this loan.

4. If you have medical bills or car repairs, you may have to borrow the money to cover these unexpected expenses.

5. You're depending more and more on overtime pay to cover your monthly expenses.

6. You write checks and hope your paycheck is deposited soon enough so your checks will clear.

If you answered yes to any of these points, you may have hit a major roadblock, financially. You have accumulated debt that is cutting into your budget each month. So where to you go now?

You might consider visiting a consumer credit counselor or search online for debt help. Most credit counselors are nonprofit and don't charge for their services. Another place to try is www.cheapskate-monthly.com. This site provides you with helpful hints and debt calculators that can be used for a minimal charge.

Another way to steer around the debt roadblock is by using these three steps.

1. Look at your budget. Based on your spending habits, how much can you spend to pay your creditors? You have to take care of yourself first. If you try to pay your creditors before yourself, eventually you will run out of money and start using credit cards again. So establish a reasonable amount that you can afford.

2. Next, gather all of your credit card bills. Add up your total debt from creditors and people that you borrowed money from. The best way to minimize debt is to pay off those creditors that have high interest first. Then establish reasonable payments for the rest.

3. Look at all of your minimum payments or what you have to pay. You may have ten credit cards, and each one has a minimum payment of 15 dollars. It would probably be better to consolidate these into one credit card with a low interest rate for the life of the loan. This way, you could pay $150 toward the total and make a bigger dent in the debt. Beware of credit cards with low rates for six months. They usually have transfer fees and high interest rates after the special introductory period.

Here is an example of how to create a payment plan.

You plan to pay $150 each month for debt reduction. The interest rate on your MasterCard is 21%; you have a department store card that you owe $500, and $1,000 to your brother for a loan. Each month you would plan to pay $75 to MasterCard, $55 to the department store, and $20 to your brother.

Family is important and, of course, you want to keep family and finances separate if at all possible, but unless your brother is charging interest on the money he loaned you, you may be able to take longer to pay off those types of loans than the ones accumulating interest.

And remember, paying only the minimum payment will take you many years and lots of interest when you use your credit card. That is what the credit card companies are banking on. The goal is to reduce your debt as quickly as possible. Once you finish paying off one creditor, redistribute your payments to speed up paying off the rest of your creditors.

Once you've paid off your credit cards, make a vow to pay them off monthly in the future. Accumulating "plastic debt" is the road to financial destruction for many families today.

Most important, remember this long road to financial freedom and try to avoid going down it again.

Five steps to financial freedom.

1. Establish a repayment amount.

2. Evaluate your credit card bills.

3. Establish a repayment plan. Pay off higher interests first.

4. Redistribute payments when you finish paying one creditor.

5. Never use credit cards for money you don't have.

Road Money Management

Managing your money from the road can be a challenge. That is why it is extremely important to have a budget. That way, all parties—you, your significant other, and your children—know their limits.

A successful budget will allow everyone a little spending cash. Even if it is only about $10 a week, everyone needs a little breathing room.

If you are the money manager, make sure that you pay your bills on time to avoid finance charges. Also, keep an accurate check register to avoid any unnecessary overdraft charges. Don't rely on savings or money market accounts to cover you if you overspend. This lowers your savings and can be expensive in transfer fees and bank charges.

You might need to surrender the checkbook to the family member who stays at home, especially if you are gone for weeks at a time. This does not mean that you give up any authority over your finances. It just means that you recognize that it is better for everyone to let someone else manage the money.

Once again, it is important to know how much you can spend on the road. So don't just turn over your paycheck. Stay involved. Know where your money goes.

Investing

Okay, so now you're headed in the right direction. You are successfully managing your money and are actually saving a little. Let's take a look at what the map tells us to do next.

Making your money grow.

So how can you get more out of the money you are saving? First, do you want long-term growth rates or quick returns? How much of a risk can you take, or how much of the money can you lose? What is your expected return? If you have absolutely no idea, you may want to talk to a financial advisor, take a class, or do some research on the Internet.

Now that you have an idea of what type of investment you are willing to make, let's look at different investments from less risk/less return to high risk/high return.

The easiest way to make your money grow is depositing it into a money market account that will generate interest. This is the safest way for your money to work for you. You can also get to your money when you need it. However, because it is the least risky, you will not get much back for your investment.

You could invest your money in a mutual fund. A mutual fund is usually an investment group that uses the money of all its investors to get larger returns on the investment. They are not as risky as stocks and usually have a higher rate of return than a money market account. Usually, you put money into a mutual fund so that your money will grow by gaining interest for a long period of time.

The disadvantage of mutual funds is that they don't give you quick returns and you usually have to leave your money in the fund for a long period of time. In fact, most mutual fund investors say they're putting their money in these kinds of funds for long periods, knowing that the market is going to jump from highs to lows and back again.

Putting money into mutual funds means you aren't going to need it for a long time and are comfortable with that money invested for a long period.

Investing in the stock market is usually the fast way to get a return on your money. It is also the riskiest. You could lose all of your money, so you should be careful and make sure you know what you are doing. Read about the stocks, take courses, or talk with an expert. The cost will soon pay for itself.

The bottom line is, whatever your age, money management and financial planning is important. Your company may have information about financial planning and money management available through the Human Resources department.

Like any professional, be sure you know where you are going and check your maps often so you are sure to be a success.

DEALING WITH GAMBLING ADDICTION

Most people have gambled at least once or twice in their life. For many, gambling is something they can live without. But for others, gambling is compulsive and can be very destructive, creating financial, marital, and legal problems.

Addictive gambling behavior can be difficult to control for long-distance truckers because they can often have long periods of down time away from home and have easy access to many casinos.

Compulsive gambling is seen as a symptom of an emotional disorder. Sufferers have an inability or unwillingness to accept reality, emotional insecurity, basic immaturity, and lack of self-esteem. They feel most comfortable when gambling. Many psychiatrists feel that the gambler has an underlying need for self-destruction.

The National Council on Problem Gambling says there are 10 questions you can ask yourself to see if you have a gambling problem.

1. Have you often gambled longer than you had planned?

2. Have you often gambled until your last dollar was gone?

3. Have thoughts of gambling caused you to lose sleep?

4. Have you used your income or savings to gamble while letting bills go unpaid?

5. Have you made repeated, unsuccessful attempts to stop gambling?

6. Have you broken the law or considered breaking the law to finance your gambling?

7. Have you borrowed money to finance your gambling?

8. Have you felt depressed or suicidal because of your gambling losses?

9. Have you been remorseful after gambling?

10. Have you gambled to get money to meet your financial obligations?

If you answered yes to any of these questions, you need to get professional help.

However, the compulsive gambler must first be willing to accept the fact that he or she is in the grips of an illness and has a desire to get well. Groups such as Gamblers Anonymous (http://www.gamblersanonymous.org) provide group therapy to overcome the problem. This provides a safe forum for gamblers to talk of their past experiences and present problems in an area where they are comfortable and accepted.

References

Al-Anon. (1988). *One day at a time in Al-Anon*. Al-Anon Family Group.

Aldrich, M. S. (1988). Study linking apnea to motor vehicle accidents. *Sleep Journal*, 487–494.

Centers for Disease Control and Prevention. (2000, June). Compliance with physical activity recommendations by walking for exercise. MMWR.

Fischer, L. (Ed.). (1983). *The essential Gandhi: His life, work and ideas*. Vintage Books.

Fuller, B. (2002). *Critical path*. St. Martin's Press.

James, L. (1997, July). Testimony before the U.S. House Subcommittee on Transportation and Infrastructure. *New York Times* and Automobile Association statistics cited.

James, L., & Nahl, D. (2000). *Aggressive driving prevention for law enforcement*. Prometheus Books.

Korelitz, J., et al. (1993, November/December). Studies of FMCSR. Health habits and risk factors among truck drivers. *American Journal of Health Promotion, 8*(2), 117–123.

Maslow, A. H. (1998). *Toward a psychology of being,* 3 ed. New York: John Wiley & Sons.

National Council on Problem Gambling. http://www.ncpgambling.org/.

National Highway Traffic Safety Administration. (2001, January). Talking points—aggressive driving prosecutor's plan. Stop Aggressive Driving, U.S. Department of Transportation.

National Institute for Occupational Safety and Health. (1999). Stress at work. U.S. Department of Health and Human Services, Pub. No. 99–101, p. 5.

Report of the National Commission on Sleep Disorders Research. (1993, January). Wake up America: A national sleep alert, executive summary and report.

Stooks, R., Guilleminault, C., & Dement, W. (1993). Sleep apnea and hypertension in commercial truck drivers. American Sleep Disorder Association and Sleep Research Society. *Sleep, 16*(8), 511–514.

Individual remarks, recollections, and stories presented in this book are the result of interviews and personal conversations collected by the authors.

Index